**TEACHER'S PET PUBLICATIONS**

LITPLAN TEACHER PACK
for
Great Expectations
based on the book by
Charles Dickens

Written by
Mary B. Collins

© 1997 Teacher's Pet Publications
All Rights Reserved

This **LitPlan** for Charles Dickens'
Great Expectations
has been brought to you by Teacher's Pet Publications, Inc.

Copyright Teacher's Pet Publications 1997
11504 Hammock Point
Berlin MD 21811

Only the student materials in this unit plan (such as worksheets,
study questions, and tests) may be reproduced multiple times
for use in the purchaser's classroom.

For any additional copyright questions,
contact Teacher's Pet Publications.

www.tpet.com

TABLE OF CONTENTS - *Great Expectations*

Introduction	9
Unit Objectives	12
Reading Assignment Sheet	13
Unit Outline	14
Study Questions (Short Answer)	17
Quiz/Study Questions (Multiple Choice)	28
Pre-reading Vocabulary Worksheets	51
Lesson One (Introductory Lesson)	69
Oral Reading Evaluation Form	92
Nonfiction Assignment Sheet	71
Writing Assignment 1	73
Writing Assignment 2/Project Assignment	75
Writing Assignment 3	90
Writing Evaluation Form	103
Vocabulary Review Activities	105
Extra Writing Assignments/Discussion ?s	107
Unit Review Activities	113
Unit Tests	117
Unit Resource Materials	149
Vocabulary Resource Materials	163

A FEW NOTES ABOUT THE AUTHOR
CHARLES DICKENS

DICKENS, Charles (1812-70). On a pier in New York Harbor in 1841 a crowd watched a tall sailing ship from England being towed to the pierhead. There was no ocean communication cable as yet and the ship brought the latest news. A question was yelled from the pier to the ship: "Is Little Nell dead?" Little Nell was the heroine in a serial called 'Old Curiosity Shop'. The latest installment was on the ship, and the people were anxious to learn how the story came out.

The author who could stir people to such excitement was Charles Dickens, then a young man of 29. The next year, on his visit to America, he received a reception second only to that of Lafayette in 1824. Six years before, with his 'Pickwick Papers', he had become the world's most celebrated writer.

Charles Dickens was born on Feb. 7, 1812, in Portsmouth. His father, John Dickens, was a minor clerk in the navy offices, a friendly man with a large family (Charles was the second of eight children) and only a moderate income. The family drifted from one poor home in London to another, each shabbier than the last. Presently John Dickens ended up in the Marshalsea Prison for debt and took his wife and younger children with him.

Meanwhile young Charles worked in a ramshackle warehouse, lived in a garret, visited his family in prison on Sundays, and felt that his life was shattered before it had begun. For a fictionalized account of his early life, read 'David Copperfield'. Then a timely inheritance restored the family to something like comfortable means, and Charles had a few quiet years at a private school.

Later he immortalized his father, for whom he always had a great love, as Mr. Micawber. When his own rising fortune and fame gave him control of a great newspaper, he put his father on the staff to preside over the dispatches and bought him a small country house. Dickens' mother, unsympathetic and unconscious of his genius, meant less to him; she begrudged his leaving work to go to school. He made her immortal as Mrs. Nickleby.

Dickens made his own career. A few years of secondary school was his basic education. He never attended college. His real education came from his reading and observation and daily experience. Except for the English novels of the 18th century, he knew little of great literature. Of history and foreign politics, he knew practically nothing. His novels all deal with his own day and his own environment, except for his two historical novels-'A Tale of Two Cities' and 'Barnaby Rudge'-and these were set in the recent past of the French Revolution and the Gordon Riots.

The qualities that made up Dickens' genius did not depend on formal education for development. Dickens had a reporter's eye for the details of daily life and a mimic's ear for the subtleties of common speech. Further, he had the artist's ability to select what he needed
from these raw materials of observation and to shape them into works of enduring merit.

Preparation for a Career
By teaching himself shorthand, Dickens secured the position of court reporter in the old Doctors' Commons, a survival from Elizabethan days that handled marriage, divorce, wills, and other "ghostly" causes. This experience gave Dickens a peculiar dislike of law that never left him; forever after it seemed either comic as in "Bardell vs. Pickwick" or terrible with tragedy as in 'Bleak House'. Dickens moved up in 1831 to the Reporters' Gallery of the "old-the unburned and unreformed-House of Commons." He also went to other cities and towns to report election speeches, transcribing his notes on the palm of his hand "by the light of a dark lantern in a post-chaise and four." This experience gave him a detailed and sometimes cynical view of government. To him the voters were often represented by the Eatanswill Election in 'Pickwick', parliamentary government by Doodle and Foodle and Coodle ('Our Mutual Friend'), and civil service by the Circumlocution Office ('Little Dorrit').

Thus equipped, Charles Dickens set out to conquer the world. The stage was his first dream. Night after night for two or three years he sat entranced with the melodrama of the London theaters-lurid with love, battle, treachery, and blue fire, in which a heroic young man would knock over 16 smugglers like ninepins. Melodrama put a stamp on Dickens for life. His characters, if they get excited, drop into the ranting language of the old Adelphi Theatre. On the other hand, Dickens' intense concentration on acting helped to give him that weird, almost hypnotic, power that he showed in the public reading of his works.

However, fate led him to a different career. He had a passion for creative writing, and he has told of his great joy, of his eyes dimmed with tears when a manuscript sent anonymously to an editor appeared in print. So he began writing sketches under the name of "Boz," the family nickname of a younger brother. To "Boz" came sudden and great success. The publishers, Chapman and Hall, had a plan for some serial pictures of cockney sportsmen, a Nimrod club, having all sorts of misadventures. The humor of the period turned very much on such horseplay. An artist named Seymour had drawn one or two pictures. They asked young "Boz" to write a set of stories to go with the pictures. Knowing nothing of sport, Dickens suggested changing the activities of the Nimrod club from sport to travel. When the publishers agreed, then, says Dickens, "I thought of Mr. Pickwick," which is all that has ever been known of the origin and genesis of one of the greatest characters in humorous literature. The young author was to receive 14 guineas (about $70) for each monthly installment.

The very week that the 'Pickwick Papers' began their monthly appearance, in April 1836, Dickens married Catherine Hogarth, one of the three pretty daughters of a newspaper associate. The young couple moved into rooms in Furnival's Inn. They did not realize that one day they would separate with bitter words because they believed they had made a love match. Dickens looked on Catherine, beautiful and silent, and saw nothing but the reflection of himself. Catherine looked at Charles and did not realize that genius and egotism often lie close together. Dickens indeed was not so much in love with Catherine as in love with love.

At first the 'Pickwick Papers' failed to sell more than a few hundred copies a month. Then the serial introduced the character of Mr. Sam Weller, polishing boots at the White Hart Inn. The narrative took off on the wings of imagination, down English lanes, past gabled inns, and along the highways as varied and as cheery as a flying coach at a gallop, and the world was at the author's feet. The phenomenal 'Pickwick Papers' and the books that followed steadily lifted young "Boz" to the height of success, from poverty to wealth, from obscurity to fame, all in a few brief years. The great novels of this period were 'Oliver Twist' (published in 1838), 'Nicholas Nickleby' (1839), 'Old Curiosity Shop' (1841), and 'Barnaby Rudge' (1841).

Dickens in America
Dickens now looked around for other worlds to conquer. America had welcomed his books from the start, in part because the lack of international copyright permitted American publishers to print them without paying him. Dickens, in his youth a radical who hated Toryism and aristocracy, longed to study America and its freedom at first hand. Leaving their four children at home, he landed with his wife in Boston in January 1842. The town blazed with excitement; society was thrilled; there were dinners, receptions, adulation. Young Dickens, dressed in a bright velvet waistcoat, reveled in his new and adoring audience and wrote home of the freedom of America and the comforts of the workers. H.W. Longfellow, William Ellery Channing, and others of the New England elite joined in the welcome. Young Dr. Oliver Wendell Holmes was one of those who helped to organize it.

Dickens found in Boston friendships that he never lost, even when bitterness and disillusion altered his view of America. From Boston he went to New York and a "Boz" ball of 3,000 people; to Philadelphia and a huge public reception; then to Baltimore and to Washington, where he met President John Tyler and the Congress; then to Richmond, which offered him a taste of Southern culture. Such was the triumphant progress of the young author, only a few years before a member of the shabby-genteel class of London.

Always ready to raise his voice in defense of a cause he believed in, Dickens spoke everywhere of the need for an international copyright agreement that would protect the rights of both American and British writers. He felt that it was unfair and unjust that American publishers should print and sell his books without permission from him and without paying him any royalties. Dickens did not speak of himself as the sole victim of this practice. He pointed out that all British authors were equally victimized; he also acknowledged that American authors, such as Edgar Allan Poe, suffered from the pirating of their works in England.

The newspapers in America attacked these forthright statements and accused Dickens of bad taste and of abusing American hospitality. In time Dickens' rosy view of America faded. The proof of his disillusion and disgust is revealed in his 'American Notes' (published in 1842), his letters to friends, and 'Martin Chuzzlewit' (1844). From Dickens' viewpoint, Americans all seemed to chew tobacco. They kept slaves, whom he never stopped to compare with the factory slaves of England. American government seemed all plunder and roguery. Then he went West, traveling as far as Cairo, Ill. His vision of the West contained nothing but foul and reeking canal boats, swamps, bullfrogs, and tobacco juice.

Dickens lacked the eye to see the pageant of America, the great epic of the settlements of the West; the eye to compare the canal boat with the raft and the scow of earlier settlers. He became peevish, impatient of small discomforts, resenting the fact that hotelkeepers dared to talk to him. He spent two weeks in Canada, consoled there by the presence of friends at the English garrison in Montreal. Then he returned home to discredit America with his pen.

Fame and Fortune
The years that followed Dickens' return from America-the middle period of his life-were filled with more activity, fame, and success. In 1851 he took a fine residence at Tavistock Square and lived in great style. His friends were the leading authors, artists, and actors of the day. Later on, his purchase of a country house at Gad's Hill fulfilled an ambition of his childhood. His books, appearing in monthly serial parts, enjoyed a popularity that slackened only to rise again. It is generally thought that 'David Copperfield', written as a serial in 1848 and 1849, when he was at the height of his powers, is the greatest of his novels. Contrasted with the 'Pickwick Papers', it shows the transition of Dickens' genius from the exuberance of youth to the somber acceptance of middle age.

One of his books, 'Dombey and Son', is a sort of epic of great sorrow. Dickens' books indeed appealed to his generation of readers as much for their tears as for their laughter.

Reformer-Journalist
Book writing did not entirely satisfy Dickens' ego. The onetime reporter wanted to be a newspaper editor. Dickens felt the need to reform all England. The way to do it, he felt, was to control and edit a great daily newspaper, where he should preside like Jupiter handing out lightning. Enthusiastic friends subscribed £100,000 and founded the Daily News. In January 1846 Dickens threw himself eagerly into the editorial chair of the fledgling publication and threw himself out again in 19 days. He found that in the newspaper business the lightning hits in two directions. So in 1850 he founded instead a weekly journal, Household Words, and carried on with it and a later magazine, All the Year Round (1859), until his death. Several of his own stories, 'Christmas Stories', 'A Tale of Two Cities', 'Great Expectations', and others ran in his magazine.

Dickens as Actor and Lecturer
Another activity, and this a special delight to him, was amateur theatricals that carried on Dickens' love of the stage. He himself had incomparable dramatic power. With it he had a great talent for management and an energy and enthusiasm that carried all before it. On May 16, 1851, at a performance that was given at the duke of Devonshire's London house for a charity, the young Queen Victoria and her Prince Consort and the duke of Wellington were in the audience. The queen came to a later performance in 1857 and graciously "commanded Mr. Dickens' presence"-an invitation of great honor-after the show. Mr. Dickens being in "farce" dress asked to be excused from appearing, thus defying all royal precedents.

To theatricals he soon added public lectures and readings from his works. This activity began after he had read one of his famous Christmas stories to a group of friends who received it enthusiastically. He made a number of successful tours in England, Scotland, and Ireland-from 1858 to 1859, 1861 to 1863, 1866 to 1867, and 1869 to 1870.

Relief in Work
Dickens separated from his wife in 1858. Georgina Hogarth, his wife's younger sister, had lived with the couple since 1842. She remained with Dickens until his death. His will provided for both women.

Dickens sought relief from a public curious about his personal life in the excitement of work. He made a second American tour in 1867 to 1868. It was an overwhelming success but extremely fatiguing. At home again, he resumed lecturing. His last appearance was in March 1870.

In retirement he struggled with his last task, 'The Mystery of Edwin Drood', a tale of night and storm and murder. The book was still unfinished on June 9, 1870, when Dickens died.

In the opinion of many, Dickens is England's greatest creative writer. The names and natures of his characters are unforgettable. His humor is unsurpassable, not only in the laughter that lies on the surface, but in the warmth of human kindliness below. His books are still being read all over the world. 'A Christmas Carol', conceived and written in a few weeks in 1843, is the ultimate, enduring Christmas myth of modern literature.

--- Courtesy of Compton's Learning Company

INTRODUCTION

This unit has been designed to develop students' reading, writing, thinking, and language skills through exercises and activities related to *Great Expectations* by Charles Dickens. It includes eighteen lessons, supported by extra resource materials.

The **introductory lesson** introduces students to one main theme of the novel through a bulletin board activity. Following the introductory activity, students are given a transition to explain how the activity relates to the book they are about to read. Following the transition, students are given the materials they will be using during the unit. At the end of the lesson, students begin the pre-reading work for the first reading assignment.

The **reading assignments** are approximately thirty pages each; some are a little shorter while others are a little longer. Students have approximately 15 minutes of pre-reading work to do prior to each reading assignment. This pre-reading work involves reviewing the study questions for the assignment and doing some vocabulary work for 8 to 10 vocabulary words they will encounter in their reading.

The **study guide questions** are fact-based questions; students can find the answers to these questions right in the text. These questions come in two formats: short answer or multiple choice. The best use of these materials is probably to use the short answer version of the questions as study guides for students (since answers will be more complete), and to use the multiple choice version for occasional quizzes. If your school has the appropriate equipment, it might be a good idea to make transparencies of your answer keys for the overhead projector.

The **vocabulary work** is intended to enrich students' vocabularies as well as to aid in the students' understanding of the book. Prior to each reading assignment, students will complete a two-part worksheet for approximately 8 to 10 vocabulary words in the upcoming reading assignment. Part I focuses on students' use of general knowledge and contextual clues by giving the sentence in which the word appears in the text. Students are then to write down what they think the words mean based on the words' usage. Part II nails down the definitions of the words by giving students dictionary definitions of the words and having students match the words to the correct definitions based on the words' contextual usage. Students should then have an understanding of the words when they meet them in the text.

After each reading assignment, students will go back and formulate answers for the study guide questions. Discussion of these questions serves as a **review** of the most important events and ideas presented in the reading assignments.

After students complete reading the work, there is a **vocabulary review** lesson which pulls together all of the fragmented vocabulary lists for the reading assignments and gives students a review of all of the words they have studied.

Following the vocabulary review, a lesson is devoted to the **extra discussion questions/writing assignments**. These questions focus on interpretation, critical analysis and personal response, employing a variety of thinking skills and adding to the students' understanding of the novel.

The **group activity** which follows the discussion questions has students working in small groups to discuss the main themes of the novel. Using the information they have acquired so far through individual work and class discussions, students get together to further examine the text and to brainstorm ideas relating to the themes of the novel.

The group activity is followed by a **reports and discussion** session in which the groups share their ideas about the themes with the entire class; thus, the entire class is exposed to information about all of the themes and the entire class can discuss each theme based on the nucleus of information brought forth by each of the groups.

There are three **writing assignments** in this unit, each with the purpose of informing, persuading, or having students express personal opinions. The first assignment is to give students the opportunity to express their own personal opinions by defining what the word "success" means to them. This also helps to set up the individual project that goes along with this unit. The second writing assignment is to inform: students write an actual plan by which they could achieve their own personal goals. The third assignment is to persuade: students persuade an employer to hire them.

This unit is actually a dual-unit. While students are getting through the reading of the book, most class time is spent on activities related to helping students fulfill their own great expectations. There is a great deal of emphasis put on how to find and keep a job. These activities include role-playing interviews, resume' writing, learning about financial planning, learning what kinds of jobs are available, and learning what education is needed and finding places to get that education.

In addition, there is a **nonfiction reading assignment**. Students are required to read a piece of nonfiction related in some way to *Great Expectations*. After reading their nonfiction pieces, students will fill out a worksheet on which they answer questions regarding facts, interpretation, criticism, and personal opinions. During one class period, students make **oral presentations** about the nonfiction pieces they have read. This not only exposes all students to a wealth of information, it also gives students the opportunity to practice **public speaking**.

The **review lesson** pulls together all of the aspects of the unit. The teacher is given four or five choices of activities or games to use which all serve the same basic function of reviewing all of the information presented in the unit.

The **unit test** comes in two formats: multiple choice or short answer. As a convenience, two different tests for each format have been included. There is also an advanced short answer unit test for higher level students.

There are additional **support materials** included with this unit. The **extra activities section** includes suggestions for an in-class library, crossword and word search puzzles related to the novel, and extra vocabulary worksheets. There is a list of **bulletin board ideas** which gives the teacher suggestions for bulletin boards to go along with this unit. In addition, there is a list of **extra class activities** the teacher could choose from to enhance the unit or as a substitution for an exercise the teacher might feel is inappropriate for his/her class. **Answer keys** are located directly after the **reproducible student materials** throughout the unit. The student materials may be reproduced for use in the teacher's classroom without infringement of copyrights. No other portion of this unit may be reproduced without the written consent of Teacher's Pet Publications, Inc.

UNIT OBJECTIVES - *Great Expectations*

1. Students will study the theme of wealth as a corrupting influence.

2. Students will demonstrate their understanding of the text on four levels: factual, interpretive, critical and personal.

3. Students will trace Pip's development through the novel to see the effects of wealth and education upon him.

4. Students will create a plan by which they could achieve their own great expectations.

5. Students will read biographical information about successful people to see how they became successful and to find role models.

6. Students will be given the opportunity to practice reading aloud and silently to improve their skills in each area.

7. Students will answer questions to demonstrate their knowledge and understanding of the main events and characters in *Great Expectations* as they relate to the author's theme development.

8. Students will enrich their vocabularies and improve their understanding of the novel through the vocabulary lessons prepared for use in conjunction with the novel.

9. The writing assignments in this unit are geared to several purposes:
    a. To have students demonstrate their abilities to inform, to persuade, or to express their own personal ideas
        Note: Students will demonstrate ability to write effectively to <u>inform</u> by developing and organizing facts to convey information. Students will demonstrate the ability to write effectively to <u>persuade</u> by selecting and organizing relevant information, establishing an argumentative purpose, and by designing an appropriate strategy for an identified audience. Students will demonstrate the ability to write effectively to <u>express personal ideas</u> by selecting a form and its appropriate elements.
    b. To check the students' reading comprehension
    c. To make students think about the ideas presented by the novel
    d. To encourage logical thinking
    e. To provide an opportunity to practice good grammar and improve students' use of the English language.

READING ASSIGNMENT SHEET - *Great Expectations*

Date Assigned	Chapters Assigned	Completion Date
	1-2	
	3-7	
	8-12	
	13-19	
	20-25	
	26-28	
	29-34	
	35-39	
	40-43	
	44-48	
	49-52	
	53-59	

UNIT OUTLINE - *Great Expectations*

1 Introduction PVR 1-2	2 Study ?s 1-2 Writing Assignment #1 PVR 3-7	3 Study ?s 3-7 Project Assignment (Writing #2) PVR 8-12	4 Study ?s 8-12 Jobs Day PVR 13-19	5 Study ?s 13-19 Jobs Day PVR 20-25
6 Study ?s 20-25 Education PVR 26-28	7 Study ?s 26-28 Education PVR 29-34	8 Study ?s 29-34 Getting a Job PVR 35-39	9 Study ?s 35-39 Job Hunting PVR 40-43	10 Study ?s 40-43 Writing Assignment #3 PVR 44-48
11 Study ?s 44-48 Resume` Writing PVR 49-52	12 Study ?s 49-52 Success PVR 53-59	13 Study ?s 53-59 Financial Planning	14 Financial Planning	15 Nonfiction Reading Library
16 Nonfiction Reading Reports	17 Vocabulary	18 Extra Discussion ?s	19 Characters	20 Project Working Session
21 Group Activity 1	22 Reports & Discussion	23 Review	24 Test	

Key: P = Preview Study Questions   V = Vocabulary Work   R = Read

STUDY GUIDE QUESTIONS

SHORT ANSWER STUDY GUIDE QUESTIONS - *Great Expectations*

Chapters 1-2
1. Identify Pip, Mrs. Joe and Joe.
2. Who does Pip meet in the graveyard?
3. What is Pip ordered to fetch under threat of losing his heart and liver?
4. Explain how Pip and Joe were "brought up by hand."
5. What did Pip do which caused him to have a guilty conscience?

Chapters 3 - 7
1. Why does Joe give Pip more gravy during dinner?
2. Joe says, "We don't know what you have done, but we wouldn't have you starved to death for it, poor miserable fellow-creature." What do we learn about Joe's character from this quote?
3. Identify Mr. Wopsle and Mr. Pumblechook.
4. What happened when Pip met the convict in the marshes the second time?
5. At the end of chapter 4, why did Pip "run for his life," and why didn't he get very far?
6. About what were the two convicts arguing when they were captured?
7. What news did Mrs. Joe bring at the end of Chapter 7?

Chapters 8 - 12
1. Identify Miss Havisham, Estella, and Biddy.
2. How does Pip describe Miss Havisham's house?
3. Why doesn't Pip tell the truth about Miss Havisham?
4. How does Pip feel about himself after his first meeting at Miss Havisham's?
5. What does Pip want from Biddy?
6. How is Pip reminded of "his convict" in the Jolly Bargemen?
7. "Pause you who read this, and think for a moment of the long chain of iron or gold, of thorns or flowers, that would never have bound you, but for the formation of the first link on one memorable day." Explain the significance of this quote.
8. Why do Camilla, Raymond and Sarah Pocket visit Miss Havisham?

Chapters 13 - 19
1. Why did Joe go to see Miss Havisham?
2. Why does Mrs. Joe get the twenty-five pounds?
3. For what purpose does Pip wish to return to Miss Havisham's after he is dismissed?
4. Why does Biddy come to live with the Gargerys?
5. Explain "Brag is a good dog, but Holdfast is a better."
6. What is Pip's great expectation?
7. Who will be Pip's tutor?
8. What did Pip want Biddy to do for Joe?

Great Expectations Short Answer Study Guide Page 2

Chapters 20 - 25
1. Identify Herbert Pocket.
2. Who are Jaggers and Wemmick?
3. Why does Pip describe the seven little Pockets as "tumbling up" instead of "growing up"?
4. Who are Startop and Drummle?
5. What did Herbert tell Pip about Estella?

Chapters 26 - 28
1. Contrast the dinner party at Jaggers' house with the one at Wemmick's.
2. Explain why Pip said, "If I could have kept him away by paying money, I certainly would have paid money."
3. Why does Joe call Pip "Sir"?
4. Joe says, "I'm all wrong in these clothes." Explain why.
5. With whom did Pip share his coach?
6. Who claimed to be the founder of Pip's fortunes?

Chapters 29 - 34
1. Who was Miss Havisham's new porter? How did Pip feel about that?
2. Why did Estella and Herbert warn Pip not to love her (Estella)?
3. Who is Mr. Waldengarver?
4. ". . . I thought of the beautiful young Estella . . . with absolute abhorrence of the contrast between the jail and her." Come back to this question later, after completing the novel, and explain why this statement is ironic.

Chapters 35 - 39
1. How do Pip and Herbert attack the problem of their debts?
2. What news did the letter from Trabb & Co. bring?
3. Why does Pip say Biddy has hurt him?
4. What did Pip receive on his birthday?
5. What did Pip do for Herbert?
6. Describe the two sides of Wemmick's character.
7. Estella says, "I am what you have made me." Explain.
8. Who is Pip's benefactor?

Chapters 40 - 43
1. What will happen to Magwitch if he is caught in England?
2. Who is Compeyson?
3. Who is Provis?
4. Why does Herbert advise Pip to get Provis out of England?
5. Of what did Drummle inform Pip?

Great Expectations Short Answer Study Guide Page 3

Chapters 44 - 48
1. Explain how Miss Havisham has used Pip.
2. What two things does Pip ask of Miss Havisham?
3. "Don't be afraid of my being a blessing to him, I shall not be that." (Estella to Pip) Explain what Estella means.
4. What does Pip find out from Wemmick?
5. What plans do Pip and Herbert make to get Magwitch out of the country?
6. What does Pip discover about Molly?

Chapters 49 - 52
1. Miss Havisham is softer and more kind when Pip visits her again. Why?
2. What tragedy happened at Miss Havisham's house?
3. How does Pip come to realize Magwitch is Estella's father?
4. What message does Pip get from Wemmick?

Chapters 53 - 59
1. Who met Pip at the "little sluice house by the limekiln"?
2. Why did Orlick try to kill Pip?
3. Trabb's boy helped Herbert and Startop find Pip. Explain why that is significant.
4. What happened to Magwitch?
5. Pip says, "I only saw him as a much better man than I had been to Joe." Explain how this shows Pip's growth as a character.
6. How does Pip treat Magwitch after his capture?
7. What happened to Pip's "great expectations"?
8. Who nurses Pip back to health?
9. Why does Joe begin calling Pip "Sir" as Pip gets better?
10. What surprises Pip when he arrives at Joe's house?
11. How does Pip carry on with his life without great expectations?
12. Is the relationship between Pip and Estella resolved? If so, how? If not, how not?

ANSWER KEY SHORT ANSWER STUDY GUIDE QUESTIONS - *Great Expectations*

Chapters 1-2

1. Identify Pip, Mrs. Joe and Joe.
   Pip is a young, orphaned boy who lives with his sister (Mrs. Joe) and her husband (Joe), a blacksmith.

2. Who does Pip meet in the graveyard?
   Pip meets a convict in the graveyard.

3. What is Pip ordered to fetch under threat of losing his heart and liver?
   The convict orders him to get a file and some food.

4. Explain how Pip and Joe were "brought up by hand."
   Mrs. Joe, Pip's sister, has a bit of a temper and dominates over both Joe and Pip. She frequently goes on a rampage at which time it is not uncommon for her to spank Pip and threaten Joe.

5. What did Pip do which caused him to have a guilty conscience?
   He took pork pie from Mrs. Joe (to give to the convict).

Chapters 3 - 7

1. Why does Joe give Pip more gravy during dinner?
   He is trying to compensate for Mr. Pumblechook's sermonizing to Pip about his character.

2. Joe says, "We don't know what you have done, but we wouldn't have you starved to death for it, poor miserable fellow-creature." What do we learn about Joe's character from this quote?
   Joe is kind-hearted and cares about others' needs. He can overlook faults and see a person as a fellow human being who should be treated with basic considerations.

3. Identify Mr. Wopsle and Mr. Pumblechook.
   Mr. Wopsle is a church clerk with theatrical tendencies.
   Mr. Pumblechook is Joe's uncle who is overbearing, pompous and hypocritical.

4. What happened when Pip met the convict in the marshes the second time?
   He gave the convict the file and food and happened to mention that there was a second convict on the loose in the marsh area, too.

5. At the end of chapter 4, why did Pip "run for his life," and why didn't he get very far?
   He thought the fact that the pork pie was missing was about to be discovered (and he knew Mrs. Joe would go on a rampage). He only got as far as the door because soldiers were there.

6. About what were the two convicts arguing when they were captured?
   One said that the other (Pip's convict) had tried to murder him.

7. What news did Mrs. Joe bring at the end of Chapter 7?
   She said that Miss Havisham wanted Pip to go "play" at her house.

Chapters 8 - 12

1. Identify Miss Havisham, Estella, and Biddy.
   Miss Havisham is an elderly spinster jilted on her wedding day. Estella is the young girl Miss Havisham has taken to raise. Biddy is the young niece of Mr. Wopsle.

2. How does Pip describe Miss Havisham's house?
   He lies and describes a velvet coach, huge dogs, and games with flags. He describes extravagance and splendor.

3. Why doesn't Pip tell the truth about Miss Havisham?
   He does not want to be misunderstood. Relating the gloom and decay she lives in seems insulting or rude to Pip, so he tells tales that do not allow a glimpse into her true life.

4. How does Pip feel about himself after his first meeting at Miss Havisham's?
   He feels coarse and common and no longer wants to be a blacksmith.

5. What does Pip want from Biddy?
   He wants her to teach him reading and writing.

6. How is Pip reminded of "his convict" in the Jolly Bargemen?
   Another convict uses Joe's file to stir his drink, and he gives Pip money, supposedly from "Pip's convict."

7. "Pause you who read this, and think for a moment of the long chain of iron or gold, of thorns or flowers, that would never have bound you, but for the formation of the first link on one memorable day." Explain the significance of this quote.
   Often, people's lives are totally changed (either for better or worse) by a single event, or a single coincidence. In Pip's case, his whole life is changed by meeting the convict in the graveyard.

8. Why do Camilla, Raymond and Sarah Pocket visit Miss Havisham?
   They visit her each year on her birthday to stay in her good graces in hopes of having a large inheritance.

Chapters 13 - 19
1. Why did Joe go to see Miss Havisham?
    She asked for him to come to discuss Pip's apprenticeship -- and to give him money as a reward for Pip's days of service to her.

2. Why does Mrs. Joe get the twenty-five pounds?
    Mrs. Joe was insulted because Miss Havisham did not invite her to come with Joe. Joe lies to her (saying Miss Havisham sent regards, etc.) and gives her the money to help keep her from going on a rampage.

3. For what purpose does Pip wish to return to Miss Havisham's after he is dismissed?
    Pip wanted to see Estella again.

4. Why does Biddy come to live with the Gargerys?
    Mrs. Joe is attacked and beaten senseless. Biddy comes to look after her and to take care of Joe and Pip.

5. Explain "Brag is a good dog, but Holdfast is a better."
    It is better to keep your word than to brag and make weak promises.

6. What is Pip's great expectation?
    He is to be educated, made a gentleman, and will come into an inheritance from a benefactor.

7. Who will be Pip's tutor?
    Matthew Pocket will be Pip's tutor.

8. What did Pip want Biddy to do for Joe?
    Pip wanted her to help educate Joe so Joe wouldn't embarrass him in his new station in life.

Chapters 20 - 25
1. Identify Herbert Pocket.
    Herbert Pocket is Pip's London flat-mate. Pip also discovers he is the "pale young gentleman" he had beaten in a fistfight at Miss Havisham's house some years before.

2. Who are Jaggers and Wemmick?
    Jaggers is a criminal lawyer and Pip's guardian. Wemmick is Jaggers' clerk.

3. Why does Pip describe the seven little Pockets as "tumbling up" instead of "growing up"?
    Their parental supervision is limited. Mrs. Pocket spends her time reading books about nobility.

4. Who are Startop and Drummle?
   Startop and Drummle are boarders at the Pocket residence. Startop is a likable fellow, but Drummle is an arrogant, unpleasant person.

5. What did Herbert tell Pip about Estella?
   He told Pip that Estella was adopted by Miss Havisham.

Chapters 26 - 28

1. Contrast the dinner party at Jaggers' house with the one at Wemmick's.
   Dinner at Jaggers' is served by the mysterious Molly, whom Wemmick had described as a tamed beast. Drummle is rude and nearly causes a fight. Dinner with Wemmick and the "Aged P" is warm and friendly.

2. Explain why Pip said, "If I could have kept him away by paying money, I certainly would have paid money."
   Pip has become a snob and is ashamed of his coarse and common roots, particularly Joe.

3. Why does Joe call Pip "Sir"?
   Joe recognizes that Pip is bettering himself and that they are no longer on the same social level. Calling Pip "Sir" is an outward sign of his respect for Pip's education.

4. Joe says, "I'm all wrong in these clothes." Explain why.
   Joe is a blacksmith, a common, uneducated man. He is at home in his old clothes, his common clothes. Dressing in "Sunday best" clothes not only makes him physically uncomfortable, it symbolizes his discomfort in a different social class, pretending (so-to-peak) to be someone he is not.

5. With whom did Pip share his coach?
   Pip shared his coach with two convicts -- one of whom had given him the two one-pound notes.

6. Who claimed to be the founder of Pip's fortunes?
   Mr. Pumblechook claimed to be the founder of his fortunes.

Chapters 29 - 34

1. Who was Miss Havisham's new porter? How did Pip feel about that?
   Orlick was the new porter. Orlick had been Joe's helper at his smith's shop. He and Pip never got along because Orlick was always jealous of Pip. Also, Orlick was suspected of being the one who attacked Mrs. Joe. With this background, Pip was naturally dismayed to find Orlick in a trusted position at Miss Havisham's house.

2. Why did Estella and Herbert warn Pip not to love her (Estella)?
   They both are fond of him and know that she is not capable of returning his love.

3. Who is Mr. Waldengarver?
   Mr. Wopsle took this as his stage name when he joined the theater.

4. ". . . I thought of the beautiful young Estella . . . with absolute abhorrence of the contrast between the jail and her." Come back to this question later, after completing the novel, and explain why this statement is ironic.
   It is ironic because Estella's own father is a convict and much of her real history is connected with jail. Also, she is in effect in a jail at Miss Havisham's house. True, she can go out and about, but the surroundings are certainly as depressing as a jail. Finally, the way Estella is raised by Miss Havisham puts her in an emotional jail, one in which she remains alone, cold, and distant from others.

Chapters 35 - 39

1. How do Pip and Herbert attack the problem of their debts?
   They sit down and make out a list of their expenditures.

2. What news did the letter from Trabb & Co. bring?
   It told of Mrs. Joe's death.

3. Why does Pip say Biddy has hurt him?
   He is hurt because she does not believe he will come more often to visit Joe now that Mrs. Joe has died.

4. What did Pip receive on his birthday?
   He got a 500 pound bonus plus a guarantee of 500 pounds per year.

5. What did Pip do for Herbert?
   He bought him a position so Herbert would have a steady income.

6. Describe the two sides of Wemmick's character.
   At Jaggers' office, Wemmick shows no humor and is strictly businesslike. His values are of how to acquire and protect "portable property." At home he is friendly, generous, and much more relaxed.

7. Estella says, "I am what you have made me." Explain.
   Estella has been raised by Miss Havisham to revenge mankind for the injustice done to her (Miss Havisham) on her wedding day. She has made Estella cold, unfeeling, and almost machine-like in her relationships with others. When Estella is cold and unfeeling towards Miss Havisham, Miss Havisham is taken aback, thinking Estella ungrateful for the years of care she has given her.

8. Who is Pip's benefactor?
   Magwitch, the convict, is Pip's benefactor.

Chapters 40 - 43
1. What will happen to Magwitch if he is caught in England?
    He will be tried, imprisoned and hanged.

2. Who is Compeyson?
    Compeyson is the other convict Pip found in the marsh. Compeyson and Magwitch, though both are convicts, are enemies.

3. Who is Provis?
    Provis is the name Magwitch assumed to protect his life upon his return to England.

4. Why does Herbert advise Pip to get Provis out of England?
    First of all, it will make it easier for Pip to break away from Magwitch without fearing for his safety (should Magwitch be offended and seek revenge). Secondly, Magwitch would really be safer out of England himself.

5. Of what did Drummle inform Pip?
    He told Pip that he was going to dine with Estella that evening.

Chapters 44 - 48
1. Explain how Miss Havisham has used Pip.
    Miss Havisham used him to make her relatives think that he would inherit a sizeable portion of her estate. Also, she used him for Estella to "practice" her ways against men. Finally, she knew he thought she was his benefactress but never told him she was not.

2. What two things does Pip ask of Miss Havisham?
    He asks for her to consider that Matthew Pocket's nature is superior to the other Pocket cousins (to remember that he is a finer person than the rest), and he asks her to give him the money for Herbert to retain his position.

3. "Don't be afraid of my being a blessing to him, I shall not be that." (Estella to Pip) Explain what Estella means.
    She meant that she would be only a shell of a wife for Drummle that emotional cold war against men had not changed; she intended to make Drummle miserable in the end.

4. What does Pip find out from Wemmick?
    Wemmick tells him that Magwitch is being hunted and that Pip's rooms are being watched.

5. What plans do Pip and Herbert make to get Magwitch out of the country?
    They will buy a boat and row up and down the river daily in order to dispel suspicion. When it is safe, they will include Magwitch on their boat and row him to a ship which will take him out of the country.

6. What does Pip discover about Molly?
    She is Estella's mother.

Chapters 49 - 52

1. Miss Havisham is softer and more kind when Pip visits her again. Why?
    The suffering she has caused Pip and the cruelty she has done to Estella have made her suffer and feel pity.

2. What tragedy happened at Miss Havisham's house?
    Miss Havisham got set on fire. Pip came back to the house and saved her (put out the fire), but she had been burned badly and so had he (on his arms and hands).

3. How does Pip come to realize Magwitch is Estella's father?
    Herbert relates what Magwitch has told him about his "missis" being tried for murdering another woman and that the case made Jaggers famous.

4. What message does Pip get from Wemmick?
    He let Pip know that it was time to take Magwitch out of the country.

Chapters 53 - 59

1. Who met Pip at the "little sluice house by the limekiln"?
    Orlick met him there.

2. Why did Orlick try to kill Pip?
    Orlick was jealous of Pip. Also, Pip had cost him his job at Miss Havisham's house and had come between him and Biddy.

3. Trabb's boy helped Herbert and Startop find Pip. Explain why that is significant.
    Trabb's boy had earlier been the source of great embarrassment for Pip, mocking him in public. It is therefore ironic that he should be one responsible for Pip's rescue. This turn of events adds to Dickens' positioning of good people with bad traits and bad people with good traits.

4. What happened to Magwitch?
    Magwitch was captured during the escape, sent to prison, and died there before he would have been executed.

5. Pip says, "I only saw him as a much better man than I had been to Joe." Explain how this shows Pip's growth as a character.
    Pip finally realizes that there is more to being a gentleman, an honorable person, than having money and education. He realizes and regrets that he treated Joe poorly, and he shows that he recognizes Magwitch was a good man although he was a convict.

6. How does Pip treat Magwitch after his capture?
   He tends to his every need and treats him with respect.

7. What happened to Pip's "great expectations"?
   They vanished. His physical fortune of land and money from Magwitch was forfeited to the state, and just as importantly, he realized that his expectations of being a gentleman with money would make him better were false.

8. Who nurses Pip back to health?
   Joe does.

9. Why does Joe begin calling Pip "Sir" as Pip gets better?
   In his weakened state, Pip is once again at Joe's level; however, as Pip gets better, his station in life as a gentleman comes back into play, and Joe feels it necessary to recognize that difference between them.

10. What surprises Pip when he arrives at Joe's house?
    Joe and Biddy were just married.

11. How does Pip carry on with his life without great expectations?
    He gets a job with the company for which Herbert works.

12. Is the relationship between Pip and Estella resolved? If so, how? If not, how not?
    The ending is ambiguous. Dickens reunites them as friends, but whether or not they marry remains unresolved.

MULTIPLE CHOICE STUDY GUIDE/QUIZ QUESTIONS - *Great Expectations*

Chapters 1-2
1. Identify Pip, Mrs. Joe, and Joe.
    A. Pip is an orphaned boy who lives with his sister (Mrs. Joe) and her husband (Joe), a blacksmith.
    B. Pip is Mrs. Joe's uncle. Mrs. Joe is the wife of Joe, a farmer.
    C. Pip is a gentleman and scholar. He rooms with Joe, a lawyer, and his wife, Mrs. Joe.
    D. Pip is a servant. He works for a wealthy woman, Mrs. Joe, and her husband, Joe.

2. Who does Pip meet in the graveyard?
    A. The minister
    B. His secret girlfriend
    C. A friend of his dead parents
    D. A convict

3. What is Pip ordered to fetch under threat of losing his heart and liver?
    A. Money and a gun
    B. A file and some food
    C. A saw and a map
    D. Dry clothes and a crowbar

4. Explain how Pip and Joe were "brought up by hand."
    A. Mrs. Joe made all of their food and clothes herself.
    B. Mrs. Joe nursed both of them back to health when they got sick.
    C. Mrs. Joe frequently spanked Pip and threatened Joe.
    D. Mrs. Joe took an active interest in everything Pip and Joe did.

5. What did Pip do which caused him to have a guilty conscience?
    A. He stole money from Joe's shop.
    B. He took pork pie from Mrs. Joe to give to the convict.
    C. He broke Mrs. Joe's favorite dish and lied about it.
    D. He told Mr. Pumblechook that his sister was cruel.

Great Expectations Multiple Choice Study Questions Page 2

<u>Chapters 3-7</u>

6. Why does Joe give Pip more gravy during dinner?
    A. He thinks Pip is too thin and needs to be fed more.
    B. He likes to do things deliberately to get Mrs. Joe angry.
    C. It is the only Christmas present Joe can afford.
    D. He is trying to compensate for Mr. Pumblechook's criticism of Pip.

7. Joe says, "We don't know what you have done, but we wouldn't have you starved to death for it, poor miserable fellow-creature." What do we learn about Joe's character from this quote?
    A. He is kind-hearted and cares about others' needs. He can overlook faults and see a person as a fellow human being who should be treated considerately.
    B. He is naive and unsuspecting. He is easily tricked, although he does not seem to get upset by it.
    C. He is overly-generous. He would unthinkingly offer his family's last bit of food to anyone who asked for it.
    D. He is secretly a rebel. He doesn't believe in the laws of England, and works in devious means to disobey them.

8. Identify Mr. Wopsle and Mr. Pumblechook.
    A. They are the co-owners of the town's tavern.
    B. Mr. Wopsle is the minister. Mr. Pumblechook is the owner of the general store.
    C. Mr. Wopsle is a church clerk. Mr. Pumblechook is Joe's uncle.
    D. Mr. Wopsle is Mrs. Joe's brother. Mr. Pumblechook is a farmer.

9. What happened when Pip met the convict in the marshes the second time?
    A. The convict was not happy with the food, and hit Pip.
    B. Pip gave the convict the food and file and mentioned that there was another convict on the loose in the marsh area.
    C. The convict said he was going to take Pip with him to help him file off the chain and escape the area.
    D. The convict thanked Pip and apologized for threatening him earlier.

Great Expectations Multiple Choice Study Questions Page 3

10. At the end of Chapter 4, why did Pip "run for his life," and why didn't he get very far?
    A. He wanted to get as far away from the convict as he could. The convict was too fast, and overtook him.
    B. He thought Mr. Pumblechook was going to beat him. He didn't get far because the door was locked.
    C. He had accidentally spilled gravy on Mrs. Hubble's dress, and was afraid of being punished. He tripped over the leg of Joe's chair.
    D. He knew Mrs. Joe would go on a rampage when she discovered the missing pork pie. There were soldiers at the door when he tried to get out.

11. About what were the two convicts arguing when they were captured?
    A. Pip's convict wouldn't let the other one use the file.
    B. The other one wanted to escape together, but Pip's convict wanted to split up.
    C. One said that the other (Pip's convict) had tried to murder him.
    D. They had different directions in mind for their escape.

12. What news did Mrs. Joe bring at the end of Chapter 7?
    A. Miss Havisham wanted Pip to go play at her house.
    B. The convict had been killed while trying to escape again.
    C. She was going to have a baby.
    D. Joe was going to get a lot of business from someone in town.

Great Expectations Multiple Choice Study Questions Page 4

Chapters 8-12

13. Identify Miss Havisham, Estella, and Biddy.
    A. Miss Havisham is the town schoolteacher. Estella is her daughter. Biddy is their housekeeper.
    B. Miss Havisham is an elderly spinster jilted on her wedding day. Estella is the young girl she has taken to raise. Biddy is Mr. Wopsle's niece.
    C. Miss Havisham is Joe's aunt. Estella is her companion. Biddy is Estella's younger, ill sister.
    D. Miss Havisham is the minister's niece. Estella is her nurse. Biddy is Estella's daughter.

14. How does Pip describe Miss Havisham's house?
    A. He says it is like a castle with gold candlesticks and marble fireplaces.
    B. He tells them it is dark, gloomy, and decaying.
    C. He describes extravagance and splendor with a velvet coach, dogs, and games with flags.
    D. He tells them it is gaudy and overdone with mirrors, a ballroom, and two rooms full of knickknacks from around the world.

15. Why doesn't Pip tell the truth about Miss Havisham?
    A. She has threatened to beat him if he does.
    B. He is afraid of being misunderstood, or thought to be insulting her.
    C. He wants Mrs. Joe to be jealous of his good fortune.
    D. He thinks he will not be allowed to return if the truth is known.

16. How does Pip feel about himself after first meeting Miss Havisham?
    A. He feels coarse and common and no longer wants to be a blacksmith.
    B. He feels lucky to have been "raised by hand" by Mrs. Joe.
    C. He is pleased that he is able to cheer up a sad person. He thinks maybe he should consider a career as a minister or doctor.
    D. He feels proud of his humble life. He resolves never to change it.

17. What does Pip want from Biddy?
    A. He wants her to visit Miss Havisham with him.
    B. He wants to live with her to escape his miserable home.
    C. He wants to know everything she knows about his parents.
    D. He wants her to teach him to read and write.

Great Expectations Multiple Choice Study Questions Page 5

18. How is Pip reminded of "his convict" at the Jolly Bargemen?
    A. The soldiers are in there. They recognize Joe as the blacksmith, and are talking about the arrest.
    B. The innkeeper has a pair of filed-apart ankle chains hanging on the wall. He says he has recently found them in the marsh.
    C. Mr. Wopsle gets drunk and starts talking about it.
    D. Another patron (also a convict) uses Joe's file to stir his drink, and gives Pip money.

19. "Pause you who read this, and think for a moment of the long chain of iron or gold, of thorns or flowers, that would never have bound you, but for the formation of the first link on one memorable day." Explain the significance of this quote with regard to Pip.
    A. He is falling in love with Estella.
    B. It is his fate to be a blacksmith because his parents are dead and he has to do what his sister wants.
    C. His whole life is changed by meeting the convict.
    D. Miss Havisham has been a bad influence on him.

20. Why do Camilla, Raymond, and Sarah Pocket visit Miss Havisham?
    A. They had promised the church pastor they would do it.
    B. They hope to get a large inheritance from her.
    C. They think she is curious and they like to gossip about her.
    D. They truly love her and wish she would recover.

Great Expectations Multiple Choice Study Questions Page 6

Chapters 13-19

21. Why did Joe go to see Miss Havisham?
    A. Pip wanted to introduce him to Estella.
    B. Mrs. Joe made him go because she was curious.
    C. She was dying and he wanted to pay his respects.
    D. She asked him to discuss Pip's apprenticeship and pay for Pip's services.

22. Why does Mrs. Joe get the twenty-five pounds?
    A. Joe does it to keep her from going on a rampage.
    B. Pip says it is rightfully hers for "bringing him up by hand."
    C. Mrs. Joe threatened to beat Joe if he kept the money.
    D. It was English law that children could not keep their own money.

23. For what purpose does Pip wish to return to Miss Havisham's after he is dismissed?
    A. He wants to see Estella again.
    B. Mrs. Joe sends him back to earn more money.
    C. He wants to have another fight with the boy in the courtyard.
    D. He hopes to talk her into adopting him.

24. Why does Biddy come to live with the Gargerys?
    A. Her uncle refuses to let her live in his house any longer.
    B. Her fiance is a blacksmith, and she wants to learn about the trade.
    C. She takes care of them after Mrs. Joe is attacked and beaten senseless.
    D. Mr. Wopsle and Mrs. Joe want her to marry Pip.

25. Explain "Brag is a good dog, but Holdfast is a better."
    A. Pip's pet is much smarter than Estella's.
    B. It is better to keep your word than to make weak promises.
    C. Brag and Holdfast are two of the dogs used to hunt escaped convicts.
    D. Confidence is good to have, but determination is better.

26. What is Pip's great expectation?
    A. He will become an excellent blacksmith and marry Biddy.
    B. Miss Havisham will employ him and let him live in her home.
    C. Mrs. Joe will die and leave him and Joe in peace.
    D. He will be educated, made a gentleman, and have a benefactor.

Great Expectations Multiple Choice Study Questions Page 7

27. Who will be Pip's tutor?
    A. Matthew Pocket
    B. Estella
    C. Biddy
    D. Mr. Wopsle

28. What did Pip want Biddy to do for Joe? Why?
    A. Care for him if Mrs. Joe died, so he would not be alone.
    B. Educate him so Pip would not be embarrassed by him.
    C. Cheer him up because he had been so oppressed by Mrs. Joe.
    D. Make a new suit of Sunday clothes because his old ones were shabby.

Great Expectations Multiple Choice Study Questions Page 8

Chapters 20-25

29. What do Pip and Herbert Pocket discover about each other?
    A. They are long-lost cousins.
    B. They are both to be tutored by Matthew Pocket.
    C. They both have secret benefactors.
    D. They had been in a fistfight together years ago at Miss Havisham's.

30. Who are Jaggers and Wemmick?
    A. Jaggers is the convict Pip aided. Wemmick is the other convict.
    B. Jaggers is Pip's flat-mate. Wemmick owns the boarding house.
    C. Jaggers is a lawyer and Pip's guardian. Wemmick is Jaggers' clerk.
    D. Jaggers is one of Matthew Pocket's students. Wemmick works for Pocket.

31. Why does Pip describe the seven little Pockets as "tumbling up" instead of "growing up"?
    A. Their parental supervision is limited. Mrs. Pocket reads and does not pay much attention to them.
    B. They are all very athletic. Mr. and Mrs. Pocket encourage their activity.
    C. They fight constantly, and knock each other down.
    D. They have all inherited a family illness that causes dizziness and loss of balance. It gets worse as they get older.

32. Who are Startop and Drummle?
    A. They are students of Matthew Pocket's. Startop is bright, but Drummle is slow-witted.
    B. They are street urchins Pip meets in London. They try to entice him to commit acts of thievery with them.
    C. They are boarders at the Pocket residence. Startop is likable, but Drummle is arrogant and unpleasant.
    D. They are flat-mates of Herbert Pocket's. Startop is independently wealthy. Drummle is studying law with Mr. Jaggers.

33. What did Herbert tell Pip about Estella?
    A. She was Miss Havisham's younger sister.
    B. She was secretly in love with Pip.
    C. She was plotting to inherit Miss Havisham's fortune.
    D. She was adopted by Miss Havisham.

Great Expectations Multiple Choice Study Questions Page 9

<u>Chapters 26-28</u>

34. Describe the dinner parties at Jaggers' house and at Wemmick's.
    A. They were both peaceful and pleasant.
    B. Drummle nearly causes a fight at Jaggers'. Dinner with Wemmick and his "Aged P" is warm and friendly.
    C. Neither was pleasant. Startop and Drummle showed bad manners at Jaggers', and the "Aged P" did not like having company at Wemmick's.
    D. Dinner at Jaggers was pleasant and rather boisterous. Pip and Wemmick did not have much in common, and Pip was uncomfortable there.

35. Explain why Pip said, "If I could have kept him away by paying money, I certainly would have paid money."
    A. Pip has become a snob and is ashamed of his coarse and common roots, especially Joe.
    B. Pip is embarrassed that he has not yet visited Joe. He thinks offering him some money may help ease the embarrassment.
    C. Pip offered Joe money instead of the visit, but Joe was proud and refused it.
    D. Pip wanted to give Joe some money, but his benefactor had said he could not share it.

36. Why does Joe call Pip "Sir"?
    A. Joe is angry and is being sarcastic.
    B. Mr. Wopsle told Joe he had to do it.
    C. It is a sign of respect for Pip's new education and social level.
    D. Joe thinks he is too old to be called a childish name like Pip.

37. Joe says, "I'm all wrong in these clothes." Explain why.
    A. Dressing in his Sunday best makes him uncomfortable, and symbolizes his discomfort in a different social class.
    B. He is jealous that Pip's clothes are of a better quality, and hopes that Pip will offer to buy him a new suit.
    C. He has lost weight since Mrs. Joe became ill, but he cannot afford new Sunday clothes. He is afraid Pip will make fun of him.
    D. Pip says he would have liked to have seen Joe in his blacksmith clothes, to remind him of the old days. Joe agrees.

Great Expectations Multiple Choice Study Questions Page 10

38. With whom did Pip share his coach?
    A. Mr. Wopsle and Joe
    B. Two convicts, one of whom had given him the two one-pound notes
    C. Estella and her chaperone
    D. Jaggers and Wemmick

39. Who claimed to be the founder of Pip's fortunes?
    A. Miss Havisham
    B. Joe and Mrs. Joe
    C. Mr. Jaggers
    D. Mr. Pumblechook

Great Expectations Multiple Choice Study Questions Page 11

Chapters 29-34

40. Who was Miss Havisham's new porter? How did Pip feel about it?
    A. Startop; Pip thought it was a good choice.
    B. Orlick; Pip thought it was dangerous for her because of his background.
    C. Herbert Pocket; Pip hoped that Miss Havisham would also become his benefactor.
    D. Drummle; Pip thought he was rude and didn't deserve the job.

41. Why did Estella and Herbert warn Pip not to love her (Estella)?
    A. They are both fond of him and know she is not capable of returning his love.
    B. They are secretly engaged and want Pip to stay out of their way.
    C. They both look down on Pip because of his common roots, and think he is not really good enough for her.
    D. They think his benefactor will stop sending money if he (Pip) falls in love before he finishes his education, and they want some of his money.

42. Who is Mr. Waldengarver?
    A. Mr. Jaggers' new associate
    B. The owner of the Blue Boar
    C. Mr. Wopsle's theater stage name
    D. The convict who gave Pip the money

Great Expectations Multiple Choice Study Questions Page 12

Chapters 35-39
43. How do Pip and Herbert attack the problem of their debts?
    A. They borrow money from Wemmick.
    B. They sit down and make a list of their expenditures.
    C. They change their lifestyle to be more prudent.
    D. They take on extra work to pay the debts.

44. What news did the letter from Trabb & Co. bring?
    A. It was an apology for the way Trabb's boy had acted towards Pip.
    B. It was an advertisement telling of a new fabric that had just arrived.
    C. It said he was moving his business to London and would like Pip to be a customer again.
    D. It told of Mrs. Joe's death.

45. Why does Pip say Biddy has hurt him?
    A. She does not believe he will come to see Joe now that Mrs. Joe has died.
    B. She has not been friendly like she used to be.
    C. She has refused to talk to him.
    D. She has insulted him about his new station in life.

46. What did Pip receive on his birthday?
    A. A new suit of clothes and a pair of boots
    B. A card and a basket of fruit from Estella
    C. A 500 pound bonus and a guarantee of 500 pounds per year
    D. The name of his benefactor

47. What did Pip do for Herbert?
    A. Pip secretly paid Herbert's debts.
    B. Pip bought him a position so Herbert would have a steady income.
    C. Pip introduced him to Estella.
    D. Pip took Herbert to a play and out to dinner.

48. Describe the two sides of Wemmick's character.
    A. At the office he is patient and polite. At home he has a bad temper and mistreats his father.
    B. At the office he is very respectful of Mr. Jaggers. At home he ridicules Jaggers and says how much he hates his work.
    C. He is industrious at the office, but very lazy at home.
    D. He thinks only of acquiring and protecting "portable property" at the office. At home he is friendly, generous, and relaxed.

Great Expectations Multiple Choice Study Questions Page 13

49. What was the subject of the disagreement between Estella and Miss Havisham?
    A. Estella wanted Miss Havisham's jewels, but Miss Havisham did not want to give them to her.
    B. Miss Havisham wants Estella to stay at the house, but Estella wants to go back to France to study. Miss Havisham says she is selfish.
    C. Estella is cold and unfeeling toward Miss Havisham. She thinks Estella is ungrateful, but Estella reminds her that she (Estella) has been raised that way by Miss Havisham.
    D. Miss Havisham wants Estella and Pip to become engaged. Estella says she doesn't want to marry someone with such common roots. Miss Havisham reminds her that she (Estella) also had common roots, and should be grateful to be guaranteed of a husband with money and position.

50. Who is Pip's benefactor?
    A. Magwitch, the convict
    B. Mr. Pumblechook
    C. Miss Havisham
    D. Joe

Great Expectations Multiple Choice Study Questions Page 14

Chapters 40-43
51. What will happen to Magwitch if he is caught in England?
    A. He will be sent out of the country.
    B. He will be tried, imprisoned, and hanged.
    C. He will have to pay taxes on all of the money he has given Pip.
    D. He will be allowed to stay, because he is now free.

52. Who is Compeyson?
    A. Pip's servant
    B. Joe's new helper
    C. Magwitch's lawyer
    D. The other convict

53. Who is Provis?
    A. The soldier who is pursuing Magwitch
    B. Wemmick's "Aged P"
    C. A young man with whom Estella has fallen in love
    D. The alias that Magwitch is using

54. What does Herbert advise Pip to do?
    A. Rent a room for Magwitch and protect him to make sure the money still comes.
    B. Go to Mr. Jaggers and ask for advice.
    C. Get Magwitch out of England, for his own safety and Pip's.
    D. Get as much of Magwitch's money as he can and then report him to the police.

55. Of what did Drummle inform Pip?
    A. He knew who Pip's benefactor was.
    B. He was leaving the city for good.
    C. He had told the Pockets about Pip's coarse upbringing.
    D. He was dining with Estella that evening.

Great Expectations Multiple Choice Study Questions Page 15

Chapters 44-48

56. Which is not one of the ways Miss Havisham has used Pip?
    A. To make her relatives think he would inherit part of her estate
    B. To seek revenge against her fiancé
    C. For Estella to practice her ways against men
    D. By letting him think she was his benefactress

57. What two things does Pip ask of Miss Havisham?
    A. To remember that Matthew Pocket is a finer person than the other cousins, and to give him the money to allow Herbert to keep his position
    B. To publicly announce that she was really his benefactor and to persuade Estella to marry him
    C. To give Estella all of her jewels and to loan him enough money to get started in a business
    D. To tell Jaggers she is not his benefactor, and to allow him to live with her

58. "Don't be afraid of my being a blessing to him, I shall not be that." What does Estella mean when she says that to Pip?
    A. Pip should think only of her and her happiness.
    B. She will marry Drummle, but intends to make him miserable.
    C. Even though she is going to marry another, Pip is still special to her.
    D. She knows she has common roots and will never really be a gentlewoman, even if she marries a gentleman.

59. What does Pip find out from Wemmick?
    A. Jaggers has helped Magwitch leave town.
    B. Jaggers has spent most of Pip's money.
    C. Herbert has gone to the police about Magwitch.
    D. Pip's rooms are being watched and Magwitch is being hunted.

60. What plans do Pip and Herbert make to get Magwitch out of the country?
    A. They will rent a carriage and drive him to Miss Havisham's house. At night they will take him to a ship docked near the marshes.
    B. They will disguise him as Pip's uncle. Pip will make plans for a trip to France, and Magwitch will accompany him.
    C. They will buy a boat and row up and down the river daily to dispel suspicion. When it is safe, they will include Magwitch on their boat and row him to a ship.
    D. They will pretend he has died, and put him in a coffin. They will take the coffin onto a ship to be buried at sea. Once on the ship, they will release Magwitch and throw the empty coffin overboard.

Great Expectations Multiple Choice Study Questions Page 16

61. What does Pip discover about Molly?
    A. She is Estella's mother.
    B. She is Miss Havisham's sister.
    C. She is secretly married to Mr. Jaggers.
    D. She is a fugitive from another country.

Great Expectations Multiple Choice Study Questions Page 17

Chapters 49-52

62. Miss Havisham is softer and more kind when Pip visits her again. Why?
    A. Mr. Jaggers has told her to be kinder.
    B. She wants to talk him into taking care of her.
    C. She realizes she has been cruel to Estella and has made Pip suffer.
    D. Estella asked her to be kind to Pip because she (Estella) had married Drummle.

63. What tragedy happened at Miss Havisham's house?
    A. Orlick broke in and beat her.
    B. She accidentally got set on fire.
    C. The house was destroyed by a storm.
    D. She fell down the stairs and broke her neck.

64. How does Pip come to realize Magwitch is Estella's father?
    A. Miss Havisham tells him while she is delirious.
    B. Jaggers tells Pip the true story.
    C. Herbert relates what Magwitch has told him about his wife, and Pip connects it to what he already knows about Molly.
    D. Pip read about it in the black book that Magwitch always carries.

65. What message does Pip get from Wemmick?
    A. He was about to be married, and wanted Pip to attend the wedding.
    B. His (Pip's) benefactor's money has been used up.
    C. Wemmick's Aged P had died.
    D. It was time to take Magwitch out of the country.

Great Expectations Multiple Choice Study Questions Page 18

Chapters 53-59

66. Who met Pip at the "little sluice house by the limekiln"?
    A. Joe
    B. Magwitch
    C. Orlick
    D. Compeyson

67. Which not a reason that Orlick tried to kill Pip?
    A. He was jealous of Pip.
    B. Pip had cost him his job at Miss Havisham's.
    C. Pip had come between him and Biddy.
    D. Drummle had paid him to get rid of Pip.

68. Trabb's boy helped Herbert and Startop find Pip. Why is this significant?
    A. He had earlier been the source of great embarrassment for Pip.
    B. He didn't like Pip.
    C. He helped Pip unintentionally.
    D. He had really liked Pip all along, but was jealous.

69. What happened to Magwitch?
    A. He escaped and lived the rest of his life in New South Wales.
    B. He was captured, sent to prison, and died there before he would have been executed.
    C. He was captured and sent to prison. Mr. Jaggers was able to get him released on the condition that he leave the country.
    D. He was shot and killed trying to escape his captors.

70. Pip says, "I only saw him as a much better man than I had been to Joe." About whom is he talking, and how does this show Pip's growth as a character?
    A. He sees Wemmick as a model for treating his elders better, because of the way he treats the Aged P.
    B. Mr. Pocket has been much more tolerant of Pip's lack of education than Pip has been of Joe's.
    C. Pip recognizes that Magwitch was a good man even though a convict.
    D. Mr. Jaggers treats Pip better when he loses Estella than Pip treated Joe when Mrs. Joe died.

Great Expectations Multiple Choice Study Questions Page 19

71. How does Pip treat Magwitch after his capture?
    A. Pip tends to his every need and treats him with respect.
    B. Pip is artificially kind in hopes of getting more money.
    C. Pip stays away because he does not want to be associated with a convict.
    D. Pip is polite, although somewhat distant.

72. What happened to Pip's 'great expectations?'
    A. Miss Havisham became his new benefactor and his expectations continued.
    B. He was able to keep all of Magwitch's fortune and became a wealthy man.
    C. He used all of Magwitch's money to pay his debts, and went back to the forge to work as a blacksmith.
    D. Magwitch's money and land went to the state, and Pip realized he would not become a gentleman.

73. Who nurses Pip back to health?
    A. Estella
    B. Joe
    C. Wemmick
    D. Mr. Pumblechook

74. Why does Joe begin calling Pip "Sir" as Pip gets better?
    A. Joe is acknowledging their different stations in life.
    B. Joe thinks it will make Pip feel better.
    C. Joe is really too hurt and angry to call Pip by his old name.
    D. Joe is not sure that Pip recognizes him yet, and doesn't want Pip to send him away.

75. What surprises Pip when he arrives at Joe's house?
    A. Joe has added two more rooms to the house.
    B. The house is still draped in mourning for Mrs. Joe.
    C. Joe and Biddy were just married.
    D. There is a "For Sale" sign on the property.

76. How does Pip carry on with his life without his great expectations?
    A. He becomes a blacksmith with Joe.
    B. He goes to work for Mr. Pumblechook.
    C. He becomes a soldier.
    D. He gets a job with the company for which Herbert works.

Great Expectations Multiple Choice Study Questions Page 20

77. Is the relationship between Pip and Estella resolved?
    A. The ending is ambiguous. They are reunited as friends, but are not married.
    B. Yes. Pip discovers that she has remarried and lives in London with her husband and children. He resolves never to see her.
    C. No. Pip writes to Estella, but we don't find out if he ever gets an answer.
    D. Yes. Estella tells him she will never remarry, and he leaves England, broken-hearted.

78. "...I thought of the beautiful young Estella ...with absolute abhorrence of the contrast between the jail and her." (refer to Chapter 32, and explain why this statement is ironic)
    A. Pip almost ends up in jail for helping Magwitch escape.
    B. Pip feels like his heart is in jail because he loves Estella and she doesn't love him.
    C. Much of Estella's real history is connected with jail.
    D. Estella turns out to be like her real father, and goes to jail.

ANSWER KEY - MULTIPLE CHOICE STUDY/QUIZ QUESTIONS
Great Expectations

1. A.	27. A.	53. D.
2. D.	28. B.	54. C.
3. B.	29. D.	55. D.
4. C.	30. C.	56. B.
5. B.	31. A.	57. A.
6. D.	32. C.	58. B.
7. A.	33. D.	59. D.
8. C.	34. B.	60. C.
9. B.	35. A.	61. A.
10. D.	36. C.	62. C.
11. C.	37. A.	63. B.
12. A.	38. B.	64. C.
13. B.	39. D.	65. D.
14. C.	40. B.	66. C.
15. B.	41. A.	67. D.
16. A.	42. C.	68. A.
17. D.	43. B.	69. B.
18. D.	44. D.	70. C.
19. C.	45. A.	71. A.
20. B.	46. C.	72. D.
21. D.	47. B.	73. B.
22. A.	48. D.	74. A.
23. A.	49. C.	75. C.
24. C.	50. A	76. D.
25. B.	51. B.	77. A.
26. D.	52. D.	78. C.

PREREADING VOCABULARY WORKSHEETS

VOCABULARY - *Great Expectations*

Chapters 1 & 2 Part I: Using Prior Knowledge and Contextual Clues
    Below are the sentences in which the vocabulary words appear in the text. Read the sentence. Use any clues you can find in the sentence combined with your prior knowledge, and write what you think the underlined words mean on the lines provided.

1. . . . he ate the bread <u>ravenously</u>.

_____

2. My sister, . . . had such a <u>prevailing</u> redness of skin that I sometimes used to wonder whether it was possible she washed herself with a nutmeg-grater instead of soap.

_____

3. She concluded by throwing me--I often served as a <u>connubial</u>--missile at Joe . . . .

_____

4. My thoughts strayed from that question as I looked <u>disconsolately</u> at the fire.

_____

5. My sister had a <u>trenchant</u> way of cutting our bread-and-butter for us that never varied.

_____

6. The wonder and <u>consternation</u> with which Joe stopped on the threshold of his bite and stared at me, were too evident to escape my sister's observation.

_____

7. At this point, Joe greatly <u>augmented</u> my curiosity by taking the utmost pains to open his mouth very wide, and to put it into the form of a word that looked to me like "sulks."

_____

Part II: Determining the Meaning   Match the vocabulary words to their dictionary definitions. If there are words for which you cannot figure out the definition by contextual clues and by process of elimination, look them up in a dictionary.

___ 1. ravenously   A. distinct; forceful, effective & vigorous
___ 2. prevailing   B. added to
___ 3. connubial   C. hungrily
___ 4. disconsolately   D. state of paralyzing dismay
___ 5. trenchant   E. most common; widespread
___ 6. consternation   F. relating to marriage
___ 7. augmented   G. gloomily

Vocabulary - *Great Expectations* Chapters 3 - 7

Part I: Using Prior Knowledge and Contextual Clues

Below are the sentences in which the vocabulary words appear in the text. Read the sentence. Use any clues you can find in the sentence combined with your prior knowledge, and write what you think the underlined words mean on the lines provided.

1. One black ox . . . fixed me so <u>obstinately</u> with his eyes, and moved his blunt head round in such an accusatory manner as I moved round, that I blubbered out to him, "I couldn't help it, sir!"

___

2. He shivered all the while . . . . "I think you have got the <u>ague</u>," said I.

___

3. So, we had our slices served out, as if we were two thousand troops on a forced march instead of a man and a boy at home; and we took gulps of milk and water, with apologetic <u>countenances</u>, from a jug on the dresser.

___

4. On the present festive occasion he emerged from his room, when the <u>blithe</u> bells were going . . . .

___

5. But, Uncle Pumblechook, who was <u>omnipotent</u> in that kitchen, wouldn't hear the word, wouldn't hear of the subject, imperiously waved it all away with his hand . . . .

___

6. Surrender, you two! and confound you for two wild beasts! Come <u>asunder</u>!

___

7. Both were bleeding and panting and <u>execrating</u> and struggling . . . .

___

8. My state of mind regarding the pilfering from which I had been so unexpectedly <u>exonerated</u>, did not impel me to frank disclosure . . . .

___

9. I <u>sagaciously</u> observed, if it didn't signify to him, to whom did it signify?

___

Vocabulary - *Great Expectations* Chapters 3 - 7 Continued

Part II: Determining the Meaning   Match the vocabulary words to their dictionary definitions. If there are words for which you cannot figure out the definition by contextual clues and by process of elimination, look them up in a dictionary.

___ 8. obstinately
___ 9. ague
___ 10. countenances
___ 11. blithe
___ 12. omnipotent
___ 13. asunder
___ 14. execrating
___ 15. exonerated
___ 16. sagaciously

A. carefree & lighthearted
B. faces
C. all-powerful
D. stubbornly
E. cursing
F. intelligently; wisely
G. fever and chills
H. apart from each other
I. freed from blame

Vocabulary - *Great Expectations* Chapters 8 - 12

Part I: Using Prior Knowledge and Contextual Clues

Below are the sentences in which the vocabulary words appear in the text. Read the sentence. Use any clues you can find in the sentence combined with your prior knowledge, and write what you think the underlined words mean on the lines provided.

1. She put the mug down on the stones of the yard, and gave me the bread and meat without looking at me, as insolently as if I were a dog in disgrace.

___

2. I had known . . . that my sister, in her capricious and violent coercion, was unjust to me.

___

3. And I soon found myself getting heavily bumped from behind in the nape of the neck and the small of the back, and having my face ignominiously shoved against the kitchen wall, because I did not answer those questions at sufficient length.

___

4. The felicitous idea occurred to me, a morning or two later when I woke, that the best step I could take towards making myself uncommon was to get out of Biddy everything she knew.

___

5. The Educational scheme or Course established by Mr. Wopsle's great-aunt may be resolved into the following synopsis.

___

6. When this horrible din had lasted a certain time, it mechanically awoke Mr. Wopsle's great-aunt, who staggered at a boy fortuitously and pulled his ears.

___

7. The passage was a long one, and seemed to pervade the whole square basement of the Manor House.

___

8. . . . I even kept close at home, and looked out at the kitchen door with the greatest caution and trepidation before going on an errand, lest the officers of the County Jail should pounce upon me.

___

Vocabulary - *Great Expectations* Chapters 8 - 12 Continued

Part II: Determining the Meaning

You have tried to figure out the meanings of the vocabulary words for Chapters 8 - 12. Now match the vocabulary words to their dictionary definitions. If there are words for which you cannot figure out the definition by contextual clues and by process of elimination, look them up in a dictionary.

___ 17. insolently
___ 18. capricious
___ 19. ignominiously
___ 20. felicitous
___ 21. synopsis
___ 22. fortuitously
___ 23. pervade
___ 24. trepidation

A. lucky
B. be present throughout
C. insultingly; rudely
D. state of dread or alarm
E. whimsical
F. shamefully; humiliatingly
G. summary
H. by accident or chance

Vocabulary - *Great Expectations* Chapters 13 - 19

Part I: Using Prior Knowledge and Contextual Clues

Below are the sentences in which the vocabulary words appear in the text. Read the sentence. Use any clues you can find in the sentence combined with your prior knowledge, and write what you think the underlined words mean on the lines provided.

1. At breakfast time my sister declared her intention of going to town with us, and being left at Uncle Pumblechook's, and called for 'when we had done with our fine ladies'--a way of putting the case, from which Joe appeared inclined to <u>augur</u> the worst.

   _____

2. One person of a mild and <u>benevolent</u> aspect even gave me a tract ornamented with a woodcut of a malevolent young man . . . .

   _____

3. He always slouched, locomotively, with his eyes on the ground; and, when accosted or otherwise required to raise them, he looked up in a half resentful, half puzzled way, as though the only thought he ever had was, that it was rather an odd and injurious fact that he should never be thinking. This <u>morose</u> journeyman had no liking for me.

   _____

4. My sister had been standing silent in the yard, within hearing--she was a most <u>unscrupulous</u> spy and listener . . . .

   _____

5. The hue and cry going off to the Hulks, and people coming thence to examine the iron, Joe's opinion was <u>corroborated</u>.

   _____

6. . . . having led up to so much mischief, it would be now more likely than ever to <u>alienate</u> Joe from me if he believed it . . . .

   _____

7. I reflected that even in those untoward times there must have been <u>latent</u> in Biddy what was now developing . . . .

   _____

8. But after I . . . had gone through an immensity of posturing with Mr. Pumblechook's very limited dressing-glass, in the <u>futile</u> endeavor to see my legs . . . .

   _____

Vocabulary - *Great Expectations* Chapters 13 - 19 Continued

Part II: Determining the Meaning

You have tried to figure out the meanings of the vocabulary words for Chapters 13 - 19. Now match the vocabulary words to their dictionary definitions. If there are words for which you cannot figure out the definition by contextual clues and by process of elimination, look them up in a dictionary.

___ 25. augur
___ 26. benevolent
___ 27. morose
___ 28. unscrupulous
___ 29. corroborated
___ 30. alienate
___ 31. latent
___ 32. futile

A. turn away; push away
B. predict
C. having no useful result
D. present but not active; hidden
E. good
F. without a conscience or a moral code
G. melancholy; gloomy
H. supported by other evidence

Vocabulary - *Great Expectations* Chapters 20 - 25

Part I: Using Prior Knowledge and Contextual Clues
   Below are the sentences in which the vocabulary words appear in the text. Read the sentence. Use any clues you can find in the sentence combined with your prior knowledge, and write what you think the underlined words mean on the lines provided.

1. I wondered how many other clerks there were up-stairs, and whether they all claimed to have the same detrimental mastery of their fellow creatures.

_____

2. "We made the money up this morning, sir," said one of the men, submissively, while the other perused Mr. Jaggers's face.

_____

3. There was an air of toleration or depreciation about his utterance of these words, that rather depressed me . . . .

_____

4. . . . it will be magnanimous in you if you'll forgive me for having knocked you about so.

_____

5. . . . [He was] so avaricious that he locked up his cake till the mice ate it . . . .

_____

6. This is that odious Sophia's doing!

_____

7. I acquiesced, of course, knowing nothing to the contrary.

_____

Part II: Determining the Meaning
   You have tried to figure out the meanings of the vocabulary words for Chapters 20 - 25. Now match the vocabulary words to their dictionary definitions. If there are words for which you cannot figure out the definition by contextual clues and by process of elimination, look them up in a dictionary.

___ 33. detrimental   A. looked over with care
___ 34. perused   B. stingy
___ 35. depreciation   C. consented without argument
___ 36. magnanimous   D. damaging
___ 37. avaricious   E. arousing strong dislike
___ 38. odious   F. belittling
___ 39. acquiesced   G. generous in forgiving; noble

Vocabulary - *Great Expectations* Chapters 26 - 28

Part I: Using Prior Knowledge and Contextual Clues

Below are the sentences in which the vocabulary words appear in the text. Read the sentence. Use any clues you can find in the sentence combined with your prior knowledge, and write what you think the underlined words mean on the lines provided.

1. He immediately began to talk to Drummle: not at all deterred by his replying in his heavy reticent way, but apparently led on by it to screw discourse out of him.

   _____

2. Hereupon Startop took him in hand, though with a much better grace than I had shown, and exhorted him to be a little more agreeable.

   _____

3. . . . I looked forward to Joe's coming. Not with pleasure . . . no, with considerable disturbance, some mortification, and a keen sense of incongruity.

   _____

4. "For it was not," said Joe, with his old air of lucid exposition, "that my only wish were to be useful to you, I should not have had the honour of breaking wittles in the company and abode of a gentleman."

   _____

5. . . . it was poisonous and pernicious and infamous and shameful, and I don't know what else.

   _____

6. They both execrated the place in very strong language, and gradually growled themselves out, and had nothing left to say.

   _____

Part II: Determining the Meaning

You have tried to figure out the meanings of the vocabulary words for Chapters 26 - 28. Now match the vocabulary words to their dictionary definitions. If there are words for which you cannot figure out the definition by contextual clues and by process of elimination, look them up in a dictionary.

___ 40. reticent   A. at odds; not matching
___ 41. exhorted   B. easily understood
___ 42. incongruity   C. reserved
___ 43. lucid   D. denounced
___ 44. pernicious   E. urged; advised
___ 45. execrated   F. destructive; deadly

Vocabulary - *Great Expectations* Chapters 29 - 34

Part I: Using Prior Knowledge and Contextual Clues
　　Below are the sentences in which the vocabulary words appear in the text. Read the sentence. Use any clues you can find in the sentence combined with your prior knowledge, and write what you think the underlined words mean on the lines provided.

1. It was too early yet to go to Miss Havisham's, so I <u>loitered</u> into the country on Miss Havisham's side of town. . . .

_____

2. "I am serious," said Estella . . . with a darkening of her face; "if we are to be thrown much together, you had better believe it at once. No!" <u>imperiously</u> stopping me as I opened my lips.

_____

3. . . . a good fellow with <u>impetuosity</u> and hesitation, boldness and diffidence, action and dreaming, curiously mixed in him.

_____

4. It was likewise to be noted of this majestic spirit that whereas it always appeared with an air of having been out a long time and walked an immense distance, it perceptibly came from a closely <u>contiguous</u> wall.

_____

5. "I am glad to have your <u>approbation</u>, gentlemen," said Mr. Waldengarver, with an air of dignity, in spite of his being ground against the wall at the time. . . .

_____

6. If there had been time, I should probably have ordered several suits of clothes for this occasion; but as there was not, I was <u>fain</u> to be content with those I had.

_____

7. I often paid him a visit in the dark back-room in which he <u>consorted</u> with an ink-jar, a hat-peg, a coal-box, a string-box, an almanac, a desk and stool, and a ruler. . . .

_____

Part II: Determining the Meaning
　　Match the vocabulary words to their dictionary definitions. If there are words for which you cannot figure out the definition by contextual clues and by process of elimination, look them up in a dictionary.

　　___ 46. loitered　　　　　A. associated
　　___ 47. imperiously　　　 B. forcefully or passionately
　　___ 48. impetuosity　　　 C. approval
　　___ 49. contiguous　　　 D. proceeded slowly or with many stops
　　___ 50. approbation　　　 E. domineeringly; overbearingly
　　___ 51. fain　　　　　　　F. neighboring; adjacent
　　___ 52. consorted　　　　 G. pleased; willing; obliged

Vocabulary - *Great Expectations* Chapters 35 - 39

Part I: Using Prior Knowledge and Contextual Clues
Below are the sentences in which the vocabulary words appear in the text. Read the sentence. Use any clues you can find in the sentence combined with your prior knowledge, and write what you think the underlined words mean on the lines provided.

1. . . . Pumblechook . . . was . . . making <u>obsequious</u> movements to catch my attention.

_____

2. In this progress I was much annoyed by the <u>abject</u> Pumblechook, who . . . persisted as a delicate attention in arranging my streaming hatband, and smoothing my cloak.

_____

3. I had taken care to have it well understood in Little Britain, when my birthday was. . . . I would call upon him at five in the afternoon of the <u>auspicious</u> day.

_____

4. I <u>alluded</u> to the advantages I had derived in my first rawness and ignorance from his society, and I confessed that I feared I had but ill repaid them . . . .

_____

5. This left me no course but to regret that I had been "betrayed into a warmth which," and on the whole to <u>repudiate</u> as untenable, the idea that I was to be found anywhere.

_____

6. Notwithstanding my inability to settle to anything--which I hope arose out of the restless and incompleted <u>tenure</u> on which I held my means--I had a taste for reading, and read regularly . . . .

_____

7. No wisdom on earth could have given me the comfort that I should have derived from their simplicity and <u>fidelity</u>; but I could never, never, never, undo what I had done.

_____

Part II: Determining the Meaning
Match the vocabulary words to their dictionary definitions. If there are words for which you cannot figure out the definition by contextual clues and by process of elimination, look them up in a dictionary.

___ 53. obsequious   A. totally reject
___ 54. abject   B. faithfulness; loyalty
___ 55. auspicious   C. full of or showing servile compliance
___ 56. alluded   D. contemptible; miserable, wretched
___ 57. repudiate   E. period during which something is held
___ 58. tenure   F. marked by success; grand
___ 59. fidelity   G. suggested indirectly

Vocabulary - *Great Expectations* Chapters 40 - 43

Part I: Using Prior Knowledge and Contextual Clues

Below are the sentences in which the vocabulary words appear in the text. Read the sentence. Use any clues you can find in the sentence combined with your prior knowledge, and write what you think the underlined words mean on the lines provided.

1. . . . I asked the watchman, on the chance of <u>eliciting</u> some hopeful explanation as I handed him a dram at the door . . . .

_____

2. I cautioned him that I must hear no more of that; that he was not at all likely to obtain a pardon; that he was <u>expatriated</u> for the term of his natural life; and that his presenting himself in this country would be an act of felony, rendering him liable to the extreme penalty of the law.

_____

3. The imaginary student pursued by the misshapen creature he had <u>impiously</u> made, was not more retched than I, pursued by the creature who had made me . . . .

_____

4. Then you must get him out of England before you stir a finger to <u>extricate</u> yourself.

_____

5. Then, Drummle glanced at me, with an <u>insolent</u> triumph on his great-jowled face that cut me to the heart . . . .

_____

6. "I am sure it's not," said he, <u>superciliously</u> over his shoulder.

_____

Part II: Determining the Meaning

You have tried to figure out the meanings of the vocabulary words for Chapters 40 - 43. Now match the vocabulary words to their dictionary definitions. If there are words for which you cannot figure out the definition by contextual clues and by process of elimination, look them up in a dictionary.

___ 60. eliciting   A. release from an entanglement
___ 61. expatriated   B. showing haughty disdain
___ 62. impiously   C. lacking reverence, respect or dutifulness
___ 63. extricate   D. bringing out; drawing forth
___ 64. insolent   E. removed from residence in one's native land
___ 65. superciliously   F. arrogant; insulting

Vocabulary - *Great Expectations* Chapters 44 - 48

Part I: Using Prior Knowledge and Contextual Clues

Below are the sentences in which the vocabulary words appear in the text. Read the sentence. Use any clues you can find in the sentence combined with your prior knowledge, and write what you think the underlined words mean on the lines provided.

1. Pursuing the narrow intricacies of the streets which at that time tended westward near the Middlesex shore of the river . . . .

___

2. It plaited itself into whatever I thought of, as a bodily pain would have done.

___

3. She really was a most charming girl, and might have passed for a captive fairy, whom that truculent Ogre, Old Barley, had pressed into his service.

___

4. . . . he (Herbert) had Mr. Campbell consigned to him, and felt a strong personal interest in his being well cared for, and living a secluded life.

___

5. And Herbert had seen him as a predatory Tartar of comic propensities, with a face like a red brick, and an outrageous hat all over bells.

___

6. Receiving this as an intimation that it was best not to delay, I settled that I would go to-morrow, and said so.

___

Part II: Determining the Meaning

You have tried to figure out the meanings of the vocabulary words for Chapters 44 - 48. Now match the vocabulary words to their dictionary definitions. If there are words for which you cannot figure out the definition by contextual clues and by process of elimination, look them up in a dictionary.

___ 66. intricacies   A. complexities
___ 67. plaited   B. entrusted; gave over to the care of another
___ 68. truculent   C. braided
___ 69. consigned   D. hint
___ 70. propensities   E. having a tendency to fight; fierce
___ 71. intimation   F. tendencies

Vocabulary - *Great Expectations* Chapters 49 - 52

Part I: Using Prior Knowledge and Contextual Clues

Below are the sentences in which the vocabulary words appear in the text. Read the sentence. Use any clues you can find in the sentence combined with your prior knowledge, and write what you think the underlined words mean on the lines provided.

1. The nooks of ruin where the old monks had once had their <u>refectories</u> and gardens . . . .

_____

2. For, I had a <u>presentiment</u> that I should never be there again, and I felt that the dying light was suited to my last view of it.

_____

3. Therefore, fearing he should be called upon to <u>depose</u> about this destroyed child, and so be the cause of her death, he hid himself . . . .

_____

4. And seeing that Mr. Jaggers stood quite still and silent, apparently quite <u>obdurate</u>, under this appeal, I turned to Wemmick, and said, "Wemmick, I know you to be a man with a gentle heart."

_____

5. . . . they were now inflexible with one another; Mr. Jaggers being highly dictatorial, and Wemmick obstinately justifying himself whenever there was the smallest point in <u>abeyance</u> for a moment.

_____

6. It is so difficult to become clearly possessed of the contents of almost any letter, in a violent hurry, that I had to read this mysterious <u>epistle</u> again. . . .

_____

Part II: Determining the Meaning

You have tried to figure out the meanings of the vocabulary words for Chapters 49 - 52. Now match the vocabulary words to their dictionary definitions. If there are words for which you cannot figure out the definition by contextual clues and by process of elimination, look them up in a dictionary.

___ 72. refectories   A. rooms where meals are served
___ 73. presentiment   B. condition of being temporarily set aside
___ 74. depose   C. hard-hearted; not giving in to persuasion
___ 75. obdurate   D. sense that something is about to happen
___ 76. abeyance   E. letter
___ 77. epistle   F. make a statement of facts

Vocabulary - *Great Expectations* Chapters 53 - 59

Part I: Using Prior Knowledge and Contextual Clues
　　Below are the sentences in which the vocabulary words appear in the text. Read the sentence. Use any clues you can find in the sentence combined with your prior knowledge, and write what you think the underlined words mean on the lines provided.

1. There being still no answer, I went out at the door, <u>irresolute</u> what to do.

___

2. Not that Trabb's boy was of a <u>malignant</u> nature, but that he had too much spare vivacity, and that it was in his constitution to want variety and excitement at anybody's expense.

___

3. Of barges, sailing colliers, and coasting traders, there were perhaps as many as now; but, of steam-ships, great and small, not a <u>tithe</u> or a twentieth part so many.

___

4. As we approached the point, I begged him to remain in a sheltered place, while I went on to <u>reconnoitre</u>; for, it was towards it that the men had passed in the night.

___

5. But for the <u>indelible</u> picture that my remembrance now holds before me, I could scarcely believe, even as I write these words, that I saw two-and-thirty men and women put before the Judge to receive that sentence together.

___

6. Whereas the Boar had cultivated my good opinion with warm <u>assiduity</u>, when I was coming into property, the Boar was exceedingly cool on the subject now that I was going out of property.

___

7. At first Biddy gave a cry, as if she thought it was my <u>apparition</u>, but in another moment she was in my embrace.

___

Part II: Determining the Meaning
　　You have tried to figure out the meanings of the vocabulary words for Chapters 53 - 59. Now match the vocabulary words to their dictionary definitions. If there are words for which you cannot figure out the definition by contextual clues and by process of elimination, look them up in a dictionary.

___ 78. irresolute　　　A. one-tenth
___ 79. malignant　　　B. constant personal attentions
___ 80. tithe　　　　　C. ghost
___ 81. reconnoitre　　D. undecided
___ 82. indelible　　　E. make a preliminary investigation
___ 83. assiduity　　　F. disposed towards evil
___ 84. apparition　　 G. permanent

ANSWER KEY - VOCABULARY
Great Expectations

Chapters 1 - 2	Chapters 3-7	Chapter 8-12
1. C	8. D	17. C
2. E	9. G	18. E
3. F	10. B	19. F
4. G	11. A	20. A
5. A	12. C	21. G
6. D	13. H	22. H
7. B	14. E	23. B
	15. I	24. D
	16. F	

Chapters 13-19	Chapters 20-25	Chapters 26-28	Chapters 29-34
25. B	33. D	40. C	46. D
26. E	34. A	41. E	47. E
27. G	35. F	42. A	48. B
28. F	36. G	43. B	49. F
29. H	37. B	44. F	50. C
30. A	38. E	45. D	51. G
31. D	39. C		52. A
32. C			

Chapters 35-39	Chapters 40-43	Chapters 44-48	Chapters 49-52
53. C	60. D	66. A	72. A
54. D	61. E	67. C	73. D
55. F	62. C	68. E	74. F
56. G	63. A	69. B	75. C
57. A	64. F	70. F	76. B
58. E	65. B	71. D	77. E
59. B			

Chapters 53-59
78. D
79. F
80. A
81. E
82. G
83. B
84. C

DAILY LESSONS

LESSON ONE

Objectives
    1. To introduce the *Great Expectations* unit.
    2. To distribute books and other related materials
    3. To preview the study questions for chapters 1-2
    4. To familiarize students with the vocabulary for chapters 1-2
    5. To read chapters 1-2

NOTE: Prior to this class period, you need to have put up a bulletin board with pictures of people who have had successful lives. Remember in choosing your pictures that success comes in many different forms to many different people. Some suggestions: Donald Trump, Mother Theresa, Jesus, Michael Jackson, Magic Johnson, Nolan Ryan, Thomas Jefferson, Abraham Lincoln, Bill Cosby, S. E. Hinton, etc. There are literally thousands of people, past and present, from which to choose. Don't forget at least one or two pictures of average people to make the point that one does not have to be famous or rich to be successful. Some average moms and dads work hard to make a good home for their families, and that is a kind of success, too.

    If you do not have bulletin board space available, use your classroom walls or a flip-chart on an easel--or just hold the pictures up one by one for students to see.

Activity #1
    If you have not identified the pictures on your bulletin board, have students identify as many as they can and have students tell what they know about each person. After you have discussed all of the pictures, ask what all those people have in common. The answer being, of course, that they were successful, each in his/her own way.

Transition: The book we are going to be reading and working with in the next several weeks is about a young, poor boy who, through a benefactor, has great expectations for success in his future.

Activity #2
    Distribute the materials students will use in this unit. Explain in detail how students are to use these materials.

    Study Guides Students should read the study guide questions for each reading assignment prior to beginning the reading assignment to get a feeling for what events and ideas are important in the section they are about to read. After reading the section, students will (as a class or individually) answer the questions to review the important events and ideas from that section of the book. Students should keep the study guides as study materials for the unit test.

Vocabulary   Prior to reading a reading assignment, students will do vocabulary work related to the section of the book they are about to read. Following the completion of the reading of the book, there will be a vocabulary review of all the words used in the vocabulary assignments. Students should keep their vocabulary work as study materials for the unit test.

Reading Assignment Sheet   You need to fill in the reading assignment sheet to let students know by when their reading has to be completed. You can either write the assignment sheet up on a side blackboard or bulletin board and leave it there for students to see each day, or you can "ditto" copies for each student to have. In either case, you should advise students to become very familiar with the reading assignments so they know what is expected of them.

Extra Activities Center   The Extra Activities Packet portion of this unit contains suggestions for an extra library of related books and articles in your classroom as well as crossword and word search puzzles. Make an extra activities center in your room where you will keep these materials for students to use. (Bring the books and articles in from the library and keep several copies of the puzzles on hand.) Explain to students that these materials are available for students to use when they finish reading assignments or other class work early.

Nonfiction Assignment Sheet   Explain to students that they each are to read at least one non-fiction piece during the unit. Students will fill out a nonfiction assignment sheet after completing the reading to help you evaluate their reading experiences and to help the students think about and evaluate their own reading experiences.

Books   Each school has its own rules and regulations regarding student use of school books. Advise students of the procedures that are normal for your school.

Activity #3
    Students should preview the study questions, do the vocabulary work, and read Chapters 1-2 of *Great Expectations* prior to your next class period.

NONFICTION ASSIGNMENT SHEET
(To be completed after reading the required nonfiction article)

Name _____ Date _____

Title of Nonfiction Read _____

Written By _____ Publication Date _____

I. Factual Summary: Write a short summary of the piece you read.

II. Vocabulary
    1. With which vocabulary words in the piece did you encounter some degree of difficulty?

    2. How did you resolve your lack of understanding with these words?

III. Interpretation: What was the main point the author wanted you to get from reading his work?

IV. Criticism
    1. With which points of the piece did you agree or find easy to accept? Why?

    2. With which points of the piece did you disagree or find difficult to believe? Why?

V. Personal Response: What do you think about this piece? OR How does this piece influence your ideas?

LESSON TWO

Objectives
1. To review the main ideas and events of chapters 1-2
2. To give students the opportunity to define and express their own opinions about what "success" is
3. To give the teacher the opportunity to evaluate students' writing
4. To preview the study questions, do the vocabulary work and read chapters 3-7

Activity #1

Give students a few minutes to formulate answers for the study guide questions for chapters 1-2, and then discuss the answers to the questions in detail. Write the answers on the board or overhead transparency so students can have the correct answers for study purposes. Note: It is a good practice in public speaking and leadership skills for individual students to take charge of leading the discussions of the study questions. Perhaps a different student could go to the front of the class and lead the discussion each day that the study questions are discussed during this unit. Of course, the teacher should guide the discussion when appropriate and be sure to fill in any gaps the students leave.

Activity #2

Distribute Writing Assignment #1. Discuss the directions in detail and give students the remainder of this period to work on the assignment. Tell students when the composition must be turned in.

Activity #3

Tell students that prior to the next class period they should have completed the prereading and reading work for chapters 3-7.

WRITING ASSIGNMENT #1 - *Great Expectations*

PROMPT
We have spent time discussing other people's success and a variety of ideas about what it means to be "successful." Your assignment is to write a composition in which you give your own definition of "successful."

PREWRITING
Stop and think for a minute. Pretend you are old--r e a l l y old. You are looking back over your life. How will you determine whether or not your life has been successful? By what criteria will you judge yourself? <u>Those</u> are the things you want to jot down as a basis for forming your composition. Make that list now.

Next to each item on the list, jot down a few reasons <u>why</u> you have chosen that as a part of your criteria.

DRAFTING
Write an introductory paragraph in which you introduce your definition of success.

In the body of your composition, write one paragraph for each of the items on your list. Use the reasons you jotted down to support and explain the items you have chosen.

Write a concluding paragraph in which you summarize what "successful" means to you.

PROMPT
When you finish the rough draft of your paper, ask a student who sits near you to read it. After reading your rough draft, he/she should tell you what he/she liked best about your work, which parts were difficult to understand, and ways in which your work could be improved. Reread your paper considering your critic's comments, and make the corrections you think are necessary.

PROOFREADING
Do a final proofreading of your paper double-checking your grammar, spelling, organization, and the clarity of your ideas.

LESSON THREE

Objectives
    1. To review the main events and ideas from chapters 3-7
    2. To preview the study questions and do the vocabulary work for chapters 8-12
    3. To read chapters 8-12
    4. To give students the opportunity to practice writing to inform
    5. To give students the opportunity to think about and plan for their own futures
    6. To give the teacher the opportunity to evaluate students' writing

Activity #1
    Give students a few minutes to formulate answers for the study guide questions for chapters 3-7, and then discuss the answers to the questions in detail. Write the answers on the board or overhead transparency so students can have the correct answers for study purposes.

Activity #2
    Distribute the Project Assignment papers. Discuss the directions in detail and give students ample time to work.
    Note: The project assignment is also Writing Assignment 2.

Activity #3
    Tell students that prior to your next class period, they should have completed the prereading and reading work for chapters 8-12.

PROJECT ASSIGNMENT - *Great Expectations*

PROMPT

Great expectations are good to have; everyone needs to hope and dream for the future. Realizing those dreams, though, takes a plan, hard work, and a little luck. During the next couple of weeks, in conjunction with reading *Great Expectations*, we are going to take an in-depth look at how you can help to make your expectations for the future become realities. The parts of this project we will do together as a glass focus on the fact that you will probably need some sort of financial security in your future. You'll need a job--a way to make money to support yourself.

Your assignment is to create a plan for yourself in which you detail what you can do for yourself to make your life "successful," according to your own definition of that word.

Realize that things happen in life, that even our best-made plans change due to circumstances beyond our control. Sometimes, like Pip, we change, and as we change, our goals and our plans for achieving those goals change. What you are making here is not something that is carved in stone; rather, it is a clay model which you will shape and refine.

REQUIREMENTS

1. Your plan should take the form of a report with headings for the following topics:

    Goals - What do you want to achieve during your life?
    Means - What are the ways by which you could achieve your goals?
    Work - What will you do to support yourself and/or a family?
    Education - What kind of education will you need? Will it involve college, technical school, apprenticeship or some other form of education?
    The Plan - Give a step-by-step plan by which you believe you could achieve your goals.
    Considerations - What kinds of things might keep you from following your plan? How can they be overcome?
    Conclusion - What can you do to insure your success?

2. Your plan must look professional, as if it had been done by a marketing company. Why? Because in real life, the more professionally done your work is, the better your chances for success are. You might as well get used to that right now.

3. The information in your report must show that you have given the topics sincere thought. Slapping something together to say you have done the report and to get a grade is not the point of this assignment. The point is to really think about and make plans for your future.

PREWRITING

Only you can determine what your goals are for your own life. Give the matter careful consideration and jot down some notes about your thoughts. Perhaps Writing Assignment 1, making your own definition of the word "success," will help you get started.

After you determine your goals, you need to decide the best means by which you can fulfill your goals. Consider your own talents, likes and dislikes, personality traits, and situation in life. Make a list of some of the ways you can use your best assets to help you.

Great Expectations Project Assignment Page 2

     No matter what your goals are in life, you still have to *live*. That means you need food, shelter, clothing, etc. That means you need a way to earn money to buy the things you need. In turn, that generally means you need a job. We will do some in-class activities which may help you find out what kinds of jobs are available. You will then need to decide which job might be right for you. Try to choose a job that helps you fulfill your goals, gives you the financial security you need, and makes use of your talents.

     After you determine what kind of a job you think you might like, you need to determine the best way to get that job. First, what are the educational requirements? Do you need a high school diploma, a college education, technical training, or some other form of education to help you learn how to do that job? Again, we will do some in-class activities to help you find the appropriate avenue for your future education. In addition, we will do in-class activities to show you how to get and keep your job.

     You have decided what your goals are, ways in which you could achieve your goals, how to support yourself while working towards your goals, and how to get the education and other skills you need to get and keep your job. Now make a step-by-step plan of things you need to do from today on to achieve your goals. Start by making a list. When you actually write your report, translate your list into sentence/paragraph form so you can fully explain each of the steps you plan to take.

     Okay. There's your plan. Now, what could go wrong? Make a list of everything you can think of that might go wrong. Next to each item on your list, write down at least one way that problem can be overcome. When you write your report, transform your list into paragraph form. Describe the problem in the first sentence of the paragraph and then explain your solution to the problem in the remainder of the paragraph. Do this for each problem.

     Finally, make a list of things you can do yourself to help insure your own success. This is, after all, *your* life. You are the person responsible for your own success or failure. So, think of things you can do to insure your own success and jot them down. Again, use paragraph form (instead of just making a list) in your report.

DRAFTING

     Using the guidelines above, actually write out your first, rough draft of your report.

PROMPT

     When you finish the rough draft of your paper, ask a student who sits near you to read it. After reading your rough draft, he/she should tell you what he/she liked best about your work, which parts were difficult to understand, and ways in which your work could be improved. Reread your paper considering your critic's comments, and make the corrections you think are necessary. Make your final copy of your report. It should be typed, double spaced between headings and paragraphs, and single spaced within the paragraphs.

LESSON FOUR

Objectives
1. To check to see that students read chapters 8-12 as assigned
2. To review the main ideas and events from chapters 8-12
3. To preview the study questions, do the vocabulary work for, and read chapters 13-19
4. To make students aware of some of the many job possibilities available

Activity #1
Quiz - Distribute quizzes and give students about 10 minutes to complete them. (Note: The quizzes may either be the short answer study guides or the multiple choice version.) Have students exchange papers. Grade the quizzes as a class. Collect the papers for recording the grades. (If you used the multiple choice version as a quiz, take a few minutes to discuss the answers for the short answer version if your students are using the short answer version for their study guides.)

Activity #2
Tell students to think of an occupation. Quickly go around the room (using the order in which students are seated) and have each student tell the name of one occupation. Write them on the chalk board for students to copy. In this round, you will probably get most of the common professions--doctor, teacher, lawyer, construction worker, postman, etc. After each student has given you one occupation, tell students to think of and write down five more occupations which have not already been named. Give students about five minutes to do the assignment. Then, go around the room again asking students to give their responses. Write these on the board, too.

Transition: Explain to students that these are just a few of the kinds of jobs people do to make a living. There are literally thousands of ways people earn money to support themselves and their families.

Activity #3
Tell students that prior to their next class period, they must find ten adults, ask what they do for a living, and write down the responses. The adults can be family members, friends, people they stop on the street, or ten people at random chosen from the phone book. (Students who choose to "cold call" for answers should be instructed to introduce themselves, explain that they are doing an assignment for school for which they need to ask ten people what they do for a living.)

Activity #4
Tell students that also prior to the next class period they should have completed the prereading and reading work for chapters 13-19 of *Great Expectations*. Give students the remainder of the class time to begin working on this assignment.

LESSON FIVE

Objectives
1. To review the main ideas and events from chapters 13-19
2. To do the prereading and reading work for chapters 20-25
3. To continue exploring the world of jobs

Activity #1
Give students a few minutes to formulate answers to the study guide questions, and then discuss the answers to the questions in detail.

Activity #2
Have students get out their homework assignments. Again, go around the room with individual students telling the occupations they found. Write these up on the board for students to copy. After compiling the lists of occupations students have found, students will have a very large list of occupations that are available in their own communities as well as in other places.

Explain that students are to use this data to help them know about and decide on occupation(s) that may interest them. Additional information about types of careers can be found in your school's library and/or guidance office.

Activity #3
Tell students that prior to the next class period they should have previewed the study questions for, done the vocabulary for and read chapters 20-25. Students may use the remainder of this class period to begin on this assignment.

LESSON SIX

Objectives
1. To review the main ideas of chapters 20-25
2. To do the prereading and reading work for chapters 26-28
3. To further investigate career possibilities and get more specific information

Activity #1
Ask students to get out their books and some paper (not their study guides). Tell students to write down ten questions (and answers) which cover the main events and ideas in chapters 20-25.

Discuss the students' questions and answers orally, making a list of the questions with brief responses on the board. Put a star next to the students' questions and answers that are essentially the same as the study guide questions. (Be sure that all the study guide questions are answered.)

Activity #2
Explain to students that there is more to know about an occupation than a simple job description. They need to know what education/training they need to have to be able to qualify for the job. What does the job pay? Is the job paid on salary, commission, or some other structure? What benefits come with the job, if any? How is job security? What are the advantages and disadvantages of having this kind of occupation? Where are these kinds of jobs available? What hours does one have to work? Make a list of these kinds of questions on the board for students to copy down.

Tell students that within the next seven days, they must find someone who does the occupation they are most interested in, and interview that person to get answers to the questions you have just listed. The interview may be done by phone.

Activity #3
Tell students that prior to the next class period they should complete the prereading and reading work for chapters 26-28. They may have the remainder of this class period to decide on what occupations most interests them or to begin working on this assignment for chapters 26-28.

INTERVIEW ASSIGNMENT SHEET

PROMPT

You are to find a person who does the job you think you might like to do later in your life. (If you are interested in more than one job type and would like to have more information about each, please feel free to conduct as many interviews as you feel are necessary. This assignment is for <u>you</u> to help you get information you need.)

After you do the interview (either by phone or in person), you must write a summary of what you learned from the person you interviewed.

GETTING STARTED

You have decided what career most interests you. Find someone who does that job. If you don't know of anyone personally, use the yellow pages in your phone book. Look under a section directly related to the occupation you wish to find out about. Call the number listed in the phone book. Explain who you are, that you are doing a project for school, and what information you need. Ask if the person you are speaking with could connect you with someone who could help you get your information. Chances are that that person will connect you or will give you the name and number of someone else who might be able to help you. Follow the leads you get until you get to the right person who can answer your questions.

THE INTERVIEW

Your interview should go something like this:

"Hello. My name is __(fill in your name)__. I am doing a project for school, and I am trying to find out information about being a __(fill in the occupation)__. Would you mind helping me by answering a few short questions? I don't think it will take any more than five minutes of your time." (Wait for a response. If the response is positive, continue. If the person does not wish to speak with you, say, "Could I call you at another time?" If the answer is still "No," say "Thank you, anyway," and hang up. Start over again finding another person to interview.)

1. Could you describe to me exactly what you do in your job? (Jot down answers to all of these questions.)
2. What requirements are there for getting a job of this type? I mean, how much and what kind of education do I need, and/or do I need work experience?
3. What is the best way to fulfill these requirements?
4. If I were lucky enough to get a job as a __(fill in the occupation)__, how much money would I make just starting out, and how much could I hope to make after having the job and gaining experience?
5. How are __(fill in the occupation)__ s paid? Would I work on a salary, commissions, or some other payment structure?
6. Are there any insurance or retirement benefits for people who do this job? If so, what are they?
7. What hours does a __(fill in the occupation)__ usually work?
8. What are the advantages of being a __(fill in the occupation)__?
9. What are the disadvantages of being a __(fill in the occupation)__?
10. What advice would you have for a person who is interested in pursuing this occupation?

"Thank you for taking the time to help me with my project."

LESSON SEVEN

Objectives
    1. To review the main events and ideas of chapters 26-28
    2. To check to see that students did the reading assignment
    3. To assign the pre-reading, vocabulary and reading work for chapters 29-34

NOTE: The easiest way to handle giving students information about education (colleges, trade schools, etc.) is to invite the person who handles this information in your school to come speak to your class today. Let that person know that you want him/her to give your students general information about colleges (general requirements, how to apply, what kinds of colleges exist, etc.), trade schools (general requirements, how to apply, what kinds exist, etc.), and other sources of education that prepare one to enter the work force. Depending on the make-up of your class, you might want to specify approximately how many minutes should be spent on each topic. (For example, in a college prep class, you would probably want more time spent on information about colleges. In a lower-level class, you might want more time spent on information about trade schools.) Be sure to include some time for the armed services, and also allow time for questions and answers. Tell students where they can get more information.

    This sounds like a lot to get through in one class period, but the intent here is just to give students an overview of what is available and to tell them where they can get more information if/when they want it.

Activity #1
    Give students a quiz on chapters 26-28. Use either the short answer or multiple choice form of the study guide questions as a quiz so that in discussing the answers to the quiz you also answer the study guide questions. Collect the papers for grade recording.

Activity #2
    Tell students that prior to Lesson Nine (give students a day and a date) they must have completed the pre-reading, vocabulary and reading work for chapters 29-34.

Activity #3
    Introduce your guest speaker. Give him/her the remainder of the class time to speak to the students.

LESSON EIGHT

Objectives
1. To review the main ideas and events from chapters 29-34
2. To give students tips about how to get a job
3. To show students what employers are looking for in employees

NOTE: The best way to impress upon students the qualities they need to exhibit when they look for a job is to invite several employers to your classroom so they can tell students directly what things they look for in employees. This way, students get the information straight from the source, not from some textbook or someone who is not an employer.

Arrange to have several employers come to your classroom. Explain to each that you are working with students, trying to prepare them to find, get and keep meaningful employment after they leave the school system. Tell each that you are trying to line up a panel of employers who will talk to a group of students about the qualities employers look for in employees.

Activity #1
Give students a few minutes to formulate answers to the study guide questions for chapters 29-34. Discuss the answers to the questions in detail.

Activity #2
Introduce your guest speakers. Explain to students that you have invited these people to your class to talk to them about what traits employers look for in employees. Ask each employer to give a brief background about himself/herself, and to candidly tell students the traits he/she looks for in an employee, and why those traits are important. Allow time at the end for students to ask questions of the employers.

Activity #3
Tell students that prior to the next class period they should have completed the prereading and reading work for chapters 35-39.

LESSON NINE

Objectives
1. To review the main ideas and events of chapters 35-39
2. To do the prereading and reading work for chapters 40-43
3. To show students the job-hunting process

Activity #1

Discuss the answers to the study guide questions for chapters 35-39. Write the answers on the board for students to copy down for study use later.

Activity #2

Distribute the JOB HUNTING worksheet. Discuss it in detail.

Activity #3

Tell students that they are to complete the vocabulary work and the reading for chapters 40-43 prior to the next class meeting.

JOB HUNTING

Most people work for a living. We find a job we can do and get paid for it. If you want to get a job, there are certain things you can do to help yourself succeed in getting one.

FINDING A JOB

1. The most common place to find a job is through the classified advertisements in the newspaper. Employers often advertise in the "help wanted" section to find employees.
2. Another common way of finding a job is by word of mouth. Talk to people in the industry that interests you, and ask if anyone has heard of any job openings either at the present or in the near future.
3. If there is somewhere you would especially like to work, call or make an appointment to meet with the personnel manager.
4. Visit your local job placement agency.
5. If you are in school, check with your job placement office. Often employers will contact schools, looking for prospective employees.
6. Go into business for yourself. Is there something you do especially well? Get the appropriate education so you know how to run your own business, and do it!

GETTING THE JOB

You and 357 other people who read the classified ads apply for the same job. How do you increase your chances of getting that job?

1. Make sure the job you have chosen is one you feel confident you can do, and that you have fulfilled any requirements requested in the ad.

2. Respond quickly. If you are the 350th applicant, chances are that the employer has already pretty much made up his/her mind about who to hire from the other 349 applicants he/she has already seen.

3. Do your homework. Find out as much as you can about the job, the company, and the person who will be hiring (or not hiring) you. Why would it be to their advantage to hire you instead of one of the other applicants?

4. Be professional. Dress appropriately for your interview. Be confident, but not too cocky. Look the interviewer straight in the eye when you answer questions. Have a firm handshake. Don't chew gum or smoke. Give straight-forward, candid answers to questions. In your manner, act like someone in that profession would act.

5. Don't be afraid to ask questions of the employer. After all, you want to make sure this job is right for you, too, and that you fully understand what you are getting in for should you get the job.

6. Bring a resume' and letters of recommendation. On the job application there may not be room for you to fill in information that is important in showing that you are capable of doing the job. Make a resume that clearly shows your strong points. Bring letters of recommendation from former employers, teachers, or others who are respected in the community, stating how you would be an asset to the employer.

7. Bring samples of your best work, when appropriate. Show the employer what you can do.

8. Follow up. After your interview, send a "thank you" note to the interviewer, thanking him/her for his/her time and for giving you the opportunity to interview. Express your hopes that you will be working for that company soon, and should that position be filled, that he/she would keep you in mind for future opportunities with the company.

Job Hunting Page 2

KEEPING THE JOB

1. After you get the job, you need to prove to the employer that you can and will do all those things you said you could do in your interview.
2. Show up to work on time.
3. Dress appropriately for your job.
4. Take care with your work to make sure it is done correctly and in a punctual manner.
5. Don't participate in office politics or gossip. Try not to stir up any trouble; try to get along with your coworkers. Have common courtesy.
6. Go the extra mile -- do a little more than the bare requirements.
7. Take pride in your work.
8. Every day act like the work you do that day will determine whether or not you keep your job.
9. Know what your worst traits are and try to overcome them.
10. Know what your best traits are and try to use them.

WHAT THEN?

If you are happy with your job, just keep at it. If you become unhappy with your job, try to figure out why you are unhappy. See if those things that make you unhappy can be changed. If they can't, put up with them while you look for a new job. Find a new job, and start over again.

A FEW NOTES

1. If you need experience to get a particular job, but can't get hired to get experience, consider part-time volunteer work with someone who does that job just so you can get experience. Meanwhile, hold down another paying job to keep food on the table.
2. Don't expect to start at the top or for premium wages. Be satisfied to get your foot in the door. Then, after you get a job, work hard to get promoted to the position or salary you want.
3. If you don't know what you want to do when you get out of school, do your best to get as much practical, useful knowledge that can be applied to a variety of fields as you can. Having a degree in philosophy, for example, wouldn't do you much good; few philosophers are hired. Having a degree in business administration, or computer science would be useful in a variety of situations. Learning how to repair car engines or care for small children would also be useful for a variety of purposes.
4. Keep setting goals and planning and working to achieve them.
5. Remember -- YOU are responsible for your own success or failure. Don't blame the guy who works next to you or the boss or the company or society in general. Figure out what you want, and go for it!

LESSON TEN

Objectives
    1. To review the main ideas and events from chapters 40-43
    2. To do the prereading and reading work for chapters 44-48
    3. To show students how to write a resume'
    4. To have students actually write a resume'

Activity #1
    Discuss the answers to the study guide questions for chapters 40-43. Write the answers on the board for students to copy down for study use later.

Activity #2
    Tell students that prior to the next class meeting they should have done the prereading and reading work for chapters 44-48.

Activity #3
    Distribute copies of the SAMPLE RESUME' and discuss each section thoroughly.

Activity #4
    Explain to students that they are now to write a resume' of their own, using the sample as a guide. Give students the remainder of this class period to do this assignment. Be sure to tell students when their resumes will be due.

SAMPLE RESUME'

NAME:	John Doe
SOCIAL SECURITY #:	616-49-0000
ADDRESS:	1111 Name A Street A City, MD 21999
TELEPHONE:	(222)666-7777
DATE OF BIRTH:	01/01/76
AVAILABILITY:	Available for full-time employment after May 15, 1994 Willing to work evenings and/or weekends prior to May 15, 1994
EDUCATION:	Washington High School A City, MD 21999 1986-1990 Graduated with Honors State University Another City, MD 21000 1990-Present Will graduate in May 1994 with a B.A. in Computer Science
WORK EXPERIENCE:	Pizza Hut A City, MD 21999 1987-1990 Worked as a bus boy and waiter Ref: Mr. Pat Pizzaman (222)666-3456 University Store State University 1990-Present Worked stocking shelves, cash register, and currently in customer service Ref: Mrs. Susan Storemanager (222)666-7890

Resume' for John Doe Page 2

EXTRACURRICULAR:	High school band, played trumpet Yearbook staff 1989 Yearbook editor 1990 High school varsity soccer team 1988-1990 Student Government Association at State College 1992-Present
SPECIAL SKILLS:	Speak Spanish fluently Specialize in building and networking PCs
SPECIAL INTERESTS:	Baseball Travel Photography
REFERENCES:	Mrs. Ima Greatteacher Principal, City High School (222)666-1234 Mr. Hesa Businessman Small Business Corporation (222)666-4765 Col. Longtime Familyfriend Retired military (222)666-3689
NOTE:	I realize I have no experience, but I am a diligent worker, can learn most things quickly, and am willing to start at an entry-level job.

LESSON ELEVEN

Objectives:
    1. To review the main ideas and events from chapters 44-48
    2. To do the prereading and reading work for chapters 49-52
    3. To give students the opportunity to practice writing to persuade
    4. To give the teacher the opportunity to evaluate students' writing skills
    5. To help prepare students for an in-class activity in Lesson Thirteen

Activity #1
    Discuss the answers to the study guide questions for chapters 44-48. Write the answers on the board for students to copy down for study use later.

Activity #2
    Tell students that prior to the next class meeting they should have done the prereading and reading work for chapters 49-52.

Activity #3
    Distribute Writing Assignment 3. Discuss the directions in detail and give students ample time to complete the assignment.

Follow - Up: After you have graded the assignments, have a writing conference with the students. (This unit schedules one in Lesson Fifteen.) After the writing conference, allow students to revise their papers using your suggestions and corrections. Give them about three days from the date they receive their papers to complete the revision. I suggest grading the revisions on an A-C-E scale (all revisions well-done, some revisions made, few or no revisions made). This will speed your grading time and still give some credit for the students' efforts.

WRITING ASSIGNMENT #3 - *Great Expectations*

PROMPT

    Suppose that when you go for your interview, the employer says, "Ok, tell me why I should hire you." What would you say? Most people would lose a golden opportunity here by giving a short, flustered, unprepared answer. Always be ready to answer that particular question. Have the answer thought out well in advance, because if the employer does ask you that, it is your opportunity to persuade him/her to hire you. Your assignment is to choose a job for which you would like to be hired and write in a composition what your answer would be if the employer would ask you, "Why should I hire you?".

PREWRITING

    Make a list of your best traits. Are you hard working? Especially creative? Full of enthusiasm? Able to concentrate for long periods of time? Write down a list of those characteristics you have that the employer would probably consider most useful.
    Then, make a list of the knowledge and experiences you would bring with you to your job. Perhaps you don't have any experience in this particular job, but you have other job or volunteer work experiences that would help you in some way.
    Make a list of the reasons why an employer probably wouldn't hire you, and try to find ways to turn the negative things into positive things. For example, if you don't have a lot of experience, the employer would save money because he wouldn't have to pay you as much as an experienced person. You are young. That sounds like a minus, but you bring with you enthusiasm and fresh ideas, which would be a plus. You are single. That sounds like a minus because you have no ties and might be more likely to jump from job to job or move from place to place; however, you have no family commitments, so you are free to travel at a moment's notice; that's a plus. Make your own list.
    Make a list of any other reasons why the employer should hire you. Do you have any particular personal connections that might be advantageous in this business? Perhaps other members of your family are in this line of work and you have benefited from their years of experience or have learned some tricks of the trade from them. Whatever the reasons, list them.
    Look at all the information you have. Which is the most convincing reason why the employer should hire you? Save it for last. Work from your weakest arguments to your strongest arguments.

DRAFTING

    Write an introductory paragraph in which you explain why you want this job and lead up to the fact that you think you would be an asset to the company.
    In the body of your composition write a paragraph for each of the reasons why the employer should hire you. Write one paragraph for your personal traits, one paragraph for your professional knowledge or experience, one paragraph in which you take what seem to be your weak points and turn them into positive assets for the employer, and one paragraph in which you give the miscellaneous reasons the employer should hire you. You do not have to write your paragraphs in that order. Work from your weakest to your strongest arguments.
    In your concluding paragraph, simply summarize the facts that you have placed before the employer. By running all the high points back by him/her, you firmly plant your best qualities in his/her mind and end on an impressive, positive note.

PROOFREADING

    Proofread your composition for errors. Have a friend or classmate read it and offer constructive criticism. Consider the criticism and make the changes you think are appropriate.

LESSON TWELVE

Objectives:
1. To review the main ideas and events from chapters 49-52
2. To do the prereading and reading work for chapters 53-39
3. To evaluate students' oral reading

Activity #1

Discuss the answers to the study guide questions for chapters 49-52. Write the answers on the board for students to copy down for study use later.

Activity #2

Give students about ten to fifteen minutes to review the study questions and do the prereading vocabulary work for chapters 53-59.

Activity #3

Have students take turns reading orally in chapters 53-59 of *Great Expectations*. If you have not given students a grade for oral reading yet this marking period, this would be a good opportunity to do so. An evaluation form is included with this unit for your convenience.

ORAL READING EVALUATION - *Great Expectations*

Name _____ Class____ Date _____

SKILL	EXCELLENT	GOOD	AVERAGE	FAIR	POOR
Fluency	5	4	3	2	1
Clarity	5	4	3	2	1
Audibility	5	4	3	2	1
Pronunciation	5	4	3	2	1
_____	5	4	3	2	1
_____	5	4	3	2	1

Total _____ Grade _____

Comments:

LESSON THIRTEEN

Objectives:
1. To review the main ideas and events of chapters 53-59
2. To give students the feel of being on a job interview and to let them practice through role-playing

Activity #1
Discuss the answers to the study guide questions for chapters 53-59.

Activity #2
Divide your class into groups of five students. Assign one student in each group to be the employer. All the remaining students in the group will be prospective employees. On the pages which follow, you will find assignment sheets for each group. Make one copy of each of these pages and cut each page in half, separating the employer instructions from the employee instructions. Give the employer half to the one person in the group who is the employer, and give the prospective employee instructions to the remainder of the group. The employers should not let the prospective employees see their assignment sheets.

Give students (especially the prospective employees) a few minutes to collect themselves and get ready for the interviews. Ten minutes should be ample time if students work diligently.

Put the employer for Group 1 at the front of the room behind a desk. Send the prospective employees out of the room where they cannot hear what is going on inside. When the employer is ready to begin the interview, signal one of the prospective employees to come in and begin the interview. When the interview is completed, the prospective employee may take his/her seat in class, and the next prospective employee should come in. Do this for all prospective employees in Group 1. At the end of the interviews, have the class vote on which prospective employee would probably get the job. Discuss why that employee would get the job. Repeat the same steps for each of the remaining groups.

JOB INTERVIEW ASSIGNMENT SHEET - GROUP 1

EMPLOYER:

You are hiring a high school student for a part-time position as an order-taker up front at a MacDonalds fast food restaurant. You've had two such part-time people quit with no notice in the last two weeks, leaving you short-staffed. You've had it with kids, but you have no choice but to keep hiring them because the adult work force in your area is generally not available nights and weekends.

Be grumpy and generally skeptical that anything your prospective employees says is true -- especially any comments about dependability. You're tired. You're frustrated, and you wonder what in the world you have to do to get someone to show up for work and stick with the job.

Here are the questions you ask:
1. Do you have any prior experience working at a fast food restaurant?
    If yes, then ask: Where did you work, what did you do, and why did you leave?
    If no, continue with 2.
2. Do you participate in any after school activities?
3. What is your grade average?
4. Why do you want to work at MacDonalds?
5. What hours would you be able to work if you are hired?
6. How do I know that you will show up for work on time and stick with the job for more than a couple of weeks?
7. Do you have anything you want to ask or tell me?

PROSPECTIVE EMPLOYEES:

You have all seen the help wanted advertisement on the MacDonalds changeable letter sign. You have called and made arrangements to meet with the manager of your local franchise.

Each of you will be interviewed independently. Your assignment is to convince the employer to hire you. Each of you must carefully consider what questions you may be asked and what your own responses would be. Do not corroborate on this assignment. You are to work independently to come up with your own approach to the interview.

Wait quietly outside your classroom until you are called. You are NOT to discuss any aspect of this assignment with your other group members.

JOB INTERVIEW ASSIGNMENT SHEET - GROUP 2

EMPLOYER:
    You and your spouse own a small but successful drugstore. You fill prescriptions and have the usual drugstore goods, including sundries: some toys, greeting cards, seasonal items, school supplies, etc. Your son used to keep the shelves stocked for you, but he recently went away to college. You are looking for someone to stock your shelves on evenings and weekends.
    You haven't had employees outside of the family before. You're very friendly and very much the motherly/fatherly type of employer. You call the boys you interview, "Son" and the girls you interview, "Dear." Shake hands, be enthusiastic and smiling, maybe even put an arm around the prospective employee's shoulders as you guide them back to the chair where the interview will take place.
    Here are the questions you will ask:
    1. Well, Son/Dear, my boy has gone off to college. Seems like just yesterday he was scootin' around on the floor learning how to crawl. My, time flies. Anyways, we need somebody to take his place keepin' the shelves stocked. Think you'd be able to do that?
    2. That's fine. My boy was a good boy. Never got into trouble. You know what I mean? (pause) I hate to pry, but beings the kind of business we're in, I've gotta be sure the person I hire isn't the bad sort, you know. You don't have a drug problem, do you?
    3. What do you do in your spare time?
    4. Where do you live?
    5. Most of our shipments come in on Tuesdays and Fridays. Could you work after school until eight on Tuesdays and all day on Saturday? If you can't, just tell me now and save us both a lot of trouble later. I know young people have things to do some Saturdays. Ever' once and a while I suppose you could work Friday nights and Saturday mornings if you need to take Saturday afternoon off. How's that sound?
    6. What do you expect to make doing this job? How much do you expect to be paid?
    7. When could you start if I would hire you?

PROSPECTIVE EMPLOYEE:
    You saw a help wanted sign in the window of your local drugstore and called to get an interview with the owner.
    You really want a job, but you have a few restrictions about when you can work. Mondays you have piano lessons right after school. Wednesdays and Thursdays you don't have any transportation to work. Also, your mother has told you that you have to be home by 8:00 PM on school nights and no later than 10 PM on non-school nights. You're supposed to go to visit with your father one weekend each month; he picks you up at noon on Saturday and returns you home by 6:00 PM on Sunday.
    Each of you will be interviewed independently. Your assignment is to convince the employer to hire you. Each of you must carefully consider what questions you may be asked and what your own responses would be. Do not corroborate on this assignment. You are to work independently to come up with your own approach to the interview.
    Wait quietly outside your classroom until you are called. You are NOT to discuss any aspect of this assignment with your other group members.

JOB INTERVIEW ASSIGNMENT SHEET - GROUP 3

EMPLOYER:

You and your husband both work until 6PM Monday through Friday. The daycare facility that cares for your three year-old son closes at 3:30, so you need someone to watch your little boy from 3:30 until 6:00 on Mondays, Thursdays and Fridays. His grandmother has agreed to watch him on Tuesdays and Wednesdays. You exhausted all other sources and resorted to putting an ad in the paper.

You are friendly but nervous. After all, this is your first and only child, and you don't really want to leave him with a total stranger.

Here are the questions you will ask:

1. How old are you?
2. Do you have any younger brothers or sisters?
3. While you are babysitting our little boy, we expect you to be with him and watch him constantly. He is at the age where he gets into everything, and it only takes a few seconds for an accident to happen. So we expect you to watch him. If he wants to watch Sesame Street on television, the television can be turned on. Otherwise, we want the television left off. Likewise, if you need to call us or your mother for advice, that's okay, but we don't want you to use our phone to chat with your friends while you are here. Do you understand these rules, and will you follow them?
4. We will count on the person we hire to be here as promised no matter what. The daycare bus will drop our little boy off here at 3:30, and someone must be here to meet the bus; the driver won't let him off the bus without seeing someone to meet him. If for some reason you absolutely cannot be here, call me so I can make arrangements. What would you consider a reason you would not be able to come?
5. How do we know you will be a good babysitter?
6. Why do you want this job?
7. When could you start?
8. How much do you expect to be paid?

PROSPECTIVE EMPLOYEE

You read an ad in the newspaper that someone wants a babysitter a few days a week in the late afternoon until dinnertime. Your parents don't have a lot of money to buy you the extra things you want, so you thought you would get a job after school to earn some extra money for yourself. You don't really want to be tied down to a job that would last a long time each day; you do need time to do homework, practice the piano and visit with your friends.

Each of you will be interviewed independently. Your assignment is to convince the employer to hire you. Each of you must carefully consider what questions you may be asked and what your own responses would be. Do not corroborate on this assignment. You are to work independently to come up with your own approach to the interview.

Wait quietly outside your classroom until you are called. You are NOT to discuss any aspect of this assignment with your other group members.

JOB INTERVIEW ASSIGNMENT SHEET - GROUP 4

EMPLOYER:

You work for your city's Parks and Recreation Department. You are in charge of setting up a summer camp for kids in your area, and you need some 15-25 year-olds to work as camp counselors. It helps if the people you hire have had some experience with little kids, but they will be put through a training program prior to the camp's opening, so experience is not imperative. You are looking for people with enthusiasm, people who are dependable, and people with a lot of patience.

Be professional--not too friendly, but not nasty, either. You've got a job to do, and you're frankly a little tired of interviewing people.

Here are the questions you will ask:
1. Have you ever attended a summer camp yourself?
2. Do you have any little brothers or sisters?
3. What would you do if a nine year-old girl gets homesick in the middle of the night and won't stop crying?
4. What does poison ivy look like?
5. Why do you want to be a camp counselor?
6. We have several different positions available, each with different working hours. Since the kids have to be supervised at all times, one set of counselors will be responsible for the kids from 7AM to 6PM with breaks from 9AM-11AM and 2PM-4PM while students are involved with other activities. Another set of counselors will be responsible for the kids from 6PM to 7AM. Counselors in this group get no official breaks, but they will sleep in the bunkroom with the kids in case there are any problems overnight. If there are no problems, their break time will be their sleeping time. A third set of counselors will have the kids at different periods throughout the day and be responsible for doing certain activities with them for one to two hour periods. This third group of counselors will work 9AM to 5PM with one hour for lunch. Which of these shifts would you prefer if you were to be hired?
7. Do you have any questions?

PROSPECTIVE EMPLOYEE:

You're free for the summer and would like to earn some extra money. You found an advertisement for camp counselors and thought that sounded like an interesting job. You are about to go on an interview for a job as a camp counselor.

Each of you will be interviewed independently. Your assignment is to convince the employer to hire you. Each of you must carefully consider what questions you may be asked and what your own responses would be. Do not corroborate on this assignment. You are to work independently to come up with your own approach to the interview.

Wait quietly outside your classroom until you are called. You are NOT to discuss any aspect of this assignment with your other group members.

JOB INTERVIEW ASSIGNMENT SHEET - GROUP 5

EMPLOYER:

You run a seasonal t-shirt shop in a beach resort area. You need people to man the cash registers and iron decals onto t-shirts. Your primary concern is to find people who are dependable, honest, smart enough to learn to use the cash register and iron-on transfer machine without making mistakes or getting injured.

Here are the questions you will ask:
1. Have you ever worked a cash register or iron-on transfer machine before?
2. Have you ever been arrested for shoplifting?
3. How can you prove to me that you will be dependable?
4. Would you willingly take random drug or alcohol tests while you are employed by me?
5. You will work ten-hour days with an hour for lunch. This job pays $3.25 per hour plus .25 for each t-shirt you sell. If you remain in my employ for the entire 12-week season, you can earn an extra $300.00 as a bonus. Would you agree to those payment terms?
6. Do you have any questions?

- -

PROSPECTIVE EMPLOYEE:

You want a summer job. You have never had a "real" job before. You saw a help-wanted sign at a t-shirt shop and decided to apply since no prior experience was required.

Each of you will be interviewed independently. Your assignment is to convince the employer to hire you. Each of you must carefully consider what questions you may be asked and what your own responses would be. Do not corroborate on this assignment. You are to work independently to come up with your own approach to the interview.

Wait quietly outside your classroom until you are called. You are NOT to discuss any aspect of this assignment with your other group members.

JOB INTERVIEW ASSIGNMENT SHEET - GROUP 6

EMPLOYER:

You and your spouse are getting older -- you're in your late 70's, and you just can't do all the physical labor you used to be able to do. You ran a little ad in your local paper looking for a neighborhood kid to keep your lawn mowed and to do odd jobs. You're rich, but cheap and didn't want to pay one of those expensive lawn services to do the work. In addition to the lawn mowing, you have flower beds to be weeded. You also are pretty picky about how your trim work is done. The hedges have to be clipped and your sidewalks and driveway have to be kept edged. This is not just a "run over the lawn with the riding mower and call it quits" job. You want someone dependable, careful, experienced with lawnmowing equipment, and inexpensive.

Describe the job to the prospective employee, and then ask these questions:
1. Where do you live?
2. Do you take care of the yard at your house?
3. Why do you want this job?
4. How much do you think you should be paid to do this job?
5. Would you prefer to work a few afternoons after school or Saturdays until school is out?
6. After school is out for the summer, would you be willing to come do some other jobs for us, like washing the car, cleaning the storm windows and screens, painting our fence, and things like that?
7. Do you have any references?

PROSPECTIVE EMPLOYEE

You were looking for a summer job and noticed that an older couple who live on the next street over from your house advertised for someone to care for their yard. That sounded interesting, so you called the number listed and got an appointment for an interview.

Answer the questions as if you personally were applying for the job. If you would do the things that were asked, say, "yes." If you would not do those things, say, "No." Just answer each question honestly.

Each of you will be interviewed independently. Your assignment is to convince the employer to hire you. Each of you must carefully consider what questions you may be asked and what your own responses would be. Do not corroborate on this assignment. You are to work independently to come up with your own approach to the interview.

Wait quietly outside your classroom until you are called. You are NOT to discuss any aspect of this assignment with your other group members.

JOB INTERVIEW ASSIGNMENT SHEET - GROUP 7

EMPLOYER:

You work for the Federal Park Service. You are in charge of a large federal park and have been given funds to hire young people to work in your park for twelve weeks during the summer. You have several different kinds of jobs available including trash patrol, facility maintenance (painting and making picnic tables, signs, trash cans, playground equipment, etc.), trail-making (making new nature trails for visitors to use), and tour guiding (showing tourists the features of the park, the species of plants & kinds of animals, etc.).

Explain the kinds of work available to the prospective employees and then ask these questions:
1. What do you like to do in your spare time?
2. Which of the jobs I described would most interest you?
3. Do you like being outdoors? Why?
4. Do you have any experience in doing any of the kinds of activities I mentioned earlier?
5. The park is open from dawn to dusk, but you would work from 9AM to 4:30 PM with 1/2 hour for lunch. Some of the jobs require you to work on some weekends. Your work week would be 40 hours long. Would you be able to work those hours?
6. The pay is $4.50 per hour plus you have free use of all of the park facilities including the swimming pools, canoe/boat rentals, recreational facilities and special events. Do you have any questions for me?
7. Do you have any references I could call?
8. Are you still interested in doing this job?

PROSPECTIVE EMPLOYEE:

You saw a poster on the bulletin board at your school stating that the federal park in your area would be interviewing students for its Youth In Nature program. The poster instructed you to go to the federal park's administrative offices on this date to learn more about the Youth In Nature program and to have an interview. You decided to go.

You are hoping to make $2,500.00 this summer so that you can take a trip to Spain with your school's Spanish Club in the fall of your next school year.

Each of you will be interviewed independently. Your assignment is to convince the employer to hire you. Each of you must carefully consider what questions you may be asked and what your own responses would be. Do not corroborate on this assignment. You are to work independently to come up with your own approach to the interview.

Wait quietly outside your classroom until you are called. You are NOT to discuss any aspect of this assignment with your other group members.

LESSON FOURTEEN

Objectives:
1. To give students some basic advice about handling money
2. To show students how, with some financial planning, they can reach their goals

Activity #1

Congratulate your students. They all were hired by the employer with whom they interviewed in the last class period. Tell students to calculate the approximate amount of money they would have made during the term of their employment. For the jobs that were not strictly "summer jobs," calculate the earnings for a four-month period. Give students about five minutes to do the necessary calculations, and then ask students what they would have done with their money.

Activity #2

Transition: Some of you already have part-time jobs and are earning money, and most of you will be making money within the next few years. I thought this would be a good time to give you some tips about managing your money, so I invited (introduce your guest speaker) to come speak with you today.

Turn your class over to the guest speaker. Have your speaker discuss basic principles of managing money.

LESSON FIFTEEN

Objectives:
1. To have students read nonfiction relating the novel to real life
2. To show students that the American Dream of going from "rags to riches" isn't dead; there are many people today who have done just that
3. To give students role models for successful, productive lives
4. To give students individual instruction about their writing skills

Activity #1

Take students to the library to find and read stories about people who have become successful. Tell them to look in periodicals like *Nation's Business, Entrepreneur, Money,* and other business-related magazines for stories about ordinary people who have started their own businesses and become successful. Other places students could look would be in sports magazines for stories about athletes who have become successful, entertainment magazines for stories about actors/actresses/musicians who have become famous, magazines like *Time* and *Newsweek* for stories about other world leaders who are considered successful. Students should fill out their Nonfiction Assignment Sheets.

Activity #2

Call students to your desk (or some other private area) to discuss their papers from Writing Assignment 1, 2 and 3. A Writing Evaluation Form is included with this unit to help structure your conferences.

Be sure to give students a day and a date for when their revisions are due.

WRITING EVALUATION FORM - *Great Expectations*

Name _____ Date _____

    Grade _____

Circle One For Each Item:

Grammar: correct   errors noted on paper

Spelling: correct   errors noted on paper

Punctuation: correct   errors noted on paper

Legibility: excellent   good   fair   poor

_____:

_____:

Strengths:

Weaknesses:

Comments/Suggestions:

LESSON SIXTEEN

Objectives:
1. For students to learn about a wide variety of successful people
2. To give students the opportunity to practice public speaking
3. To show students that success is possible
4. To show students the traits that successful people usually have

Activity #1
  Have each student stand in front of the class and tell the class about the person he/she read about for the nonfiction reading assignment. If you have a lower level class, allow students to use their nonfiction assignment sheets or note cards. Upper level class students should be able to recall what they read in the last class period without notes.

Activity #2
  After all the reports have been given, ask students to consider all the different stories they heard. Ask students what traits all those successful people had in common. Make a list on the board. You should get responses like, "They set goals." "They worked diligently." "They never gave up." "They believed in themselves." "They kept a positive attitude."

LESSON SEVENTEEN

Objective
  To review all of the vocabulary work done in this unit

Activity
  Choose one (or more) of the vocabulary review activities listed below and spend your class period as directed in the activity. Some of the materials for these review activities are located in the Vocabulary Resource section of this unit.

NOTE: If you have not yet collected students' notes from their interviews with people in the careers of their choice, be sure to collect them in this class period or soon.

VOCABULARY REVIEW ACTIVITIES

1. Divide your class into two teams and have an old-fashioned spelling or definition bee.

2. Give each of your students (or students in groups of two, three or four) a *Great Expectations* Vocabulary Word Search Puzzle. The person (group) to find all of the vocabulary words in the puzzle first wins.

3. Give students a *Great Expectations* Vocabulary Word Search Puzzle without the word list. The person or group to find the most vocabulary words in the puzzle wins.

4. Use a *Great Expectations* Vocabulary Crossword Puzzle. Put the puzzle onto a transparency on the overhead projector (so everyone can see it), and do the puzzle together as a class.

5. Give students a *Great Expectations* Vocabulary Matching Worksheet to do.

6. Divide your class into two teams. Use the *Great Expectations* vocabulary words with their letters jumbled as a word list. Student 1 from Team A faces off against Student 1 from Team B. You write the first jumbled word on the board. The first student (1A or 1B) to unscramble the word wins the chance for his/her team to score points. If 1A wins the jumble, go to student 2A and give him/her a definition. He/she must give you the correct spelling of the vocabulary word which fits that definition. If he/she does, Team A scores a point, and you give student 3A a definition for which you expect a correctly spelled matching vocabulary word. Continue giving Team A definitions until some team member makes an incorrect response. An incorrect response sends the game back to the jumbled-word face off, this time with students 2A and 2B. Instead of repeating giving definitions to the first few students of each team, continue with the student after the one who gave the last incorrect response on the team. For example, if Team B wins the jumbled-word face-off, and student 5B gave the last incorrect answer for Team B, you would start this round of definition questions with student 6B, and so on. The team with the most points wins!

7. Have students write a story in which they correctly use as many vocabulary words as possible. Have students read their compositions orally! Post the most original compositions on your bulletin board.

LESSON EIGHTEEN

Objective
       To discuss *Great Expectations* on interpretive and critical levels

Activity
       Choose the questions from the Extra Discussion Questions/Writing Assignments which seem most appropriate for your students. A class discussion of these questions is most effective if students have been given the opportunity to formulate answers to the questions prior to the discussion. To this end, you may either have all the students formulate answers to all the questions, divide your class into groups and assign one or more questions to each group, or you could assign one question to each student in your class. The option you choose will make a difference in the amount of class time needed for this activity.

Activity #3
       After students have had ample time to formulate answers to the questions, begin your class discussion of the questions and the ideas presented by the questions. Be sure students take notes during the discussion so they have information to study for the unit test.

EXTRA WRITING ASSIGNMENTS/DISCUSSION QUESTIONS - *Great Expectations*

Interpretation

1. Explain how having Pip as the narrator affects our understanding of the events in *Great Expectations*.

2. If you were to rewrite *Great Expectations* as a play, where would you start and end each act? Explain why.

3. Where is the climax of the story?

4. Is the setting important to the story? Why or why not?

5. What are the main conflicts in the story and how are they resolved?

Critical

6. Describe Pip's relationships with each of the following characters: Joe, Biddy, Mrs. Joe, Miss Havisham, Estella, Magwitch, and Orlick.

7. Are Pip's actions believably motivated? Explain why or why not.

8. Dickens is well-known for his life-like characters. Explain how he uses them to add meaning to *Great Expectations*.

9. Characterize Charles Dickens's style of writing. How does it contribute to the value of the novel?

10. Does Pip develop or change throughout the novel? If so, how? If not, why not?

11. Explain how the title relates to the events of the novel and the themes of *Great Expectations*.

12. Explain the role of these characters in the novel: Wopsle, Pumblechook, Jaggers, Wemmick, and The Aged P. Why was each included in the story?

13. Discuss the kinds of events which happen in the country as opposed to those that happen in the city in *Great Expectations*. Can specific events be categorized in this way? What is the significance of that fact?

14. Are the characters in *Great Expectations* stereotypes? If so, explain why Charles Dickens used stereotypes. If not, explain how the characters merit individuality.

Great Expectations Extra Discussion Questions page 2

15. Discuss Dickens' use of humor in the story.

16. How does *Great Expectations* reflect mid-1800s England?

17. Discuss ways in which Dickens uses the characters and events in *Great Expectations* to show that wealth is corrupting.

18. Give several examples of coincidence from the story.

Critical/Personal Response

19. Make a list of characters from *Great Expectations*. Next to each character's name place the one adjective you believe best describes that person's personality.

20. How would the story and its effect have changed if Pip's parents had been living?

21. Make a list of the characters and identify each as a "good guy" or a "bad guy." Be prepared to justify your answers.

22. What did Pip learn by the end of the book?

23. How would the story's effect have changed if the roles of Joe and Mrs. Joe were reversed?

24. *Great Expectations* was originally published in installments for issues of a magazine. Explain what effect this had on the total work.

Personal Response

25. Did you enjoy reading *Great Expectations*? Why or why not?

26. Tell the story of Pip's great expectations in a different form. For example, write lyrics for a ballad or tell it in rap music or write a poem.

27. Have you read (or seen movies of) any other works by Charles Dickens? If so, how does *Great Expectations* compare to them?

28. What are some other "rags to riches" stories you have read?

LESSON NINETEEN

Objectives
1. To have students look more closely at character development in the novel
2. To compare and contrast several of the main characters of the novel to determine the use of the character relationships in the theme development

Activity #1
Pose the following character combinations for students to compare and contrast:
Pip/Estella
Joe/Magwitch
Compeyson/Drummle
Miss Havisham/Mrs. Joe
Jaggers/Pumblechook
Biddy/Estella
Herbert/Pip
Wemmick/Herbert
The Aged P./Bill Bailey

Take each pair one at a time. Ask students how the two are alike and then how they are different. Try to get students to draw some conclusions, stating what implications these characteristics may have upon the theme development. Jot down notes on the board for students to copy for study purposes.

NOTE: This activity could also be done in groups. Assign one pair of characters per group of students. Give the groups time to discuss the characters and to make some implications before drawing the class together and asking each group to report.

Activity #2
Have students look at Pip's development throughout the novel and plot his growing points to show what effect his adventures have upon his development.

NOTE: Remind students to bring their project materials to your next class meeting.

LESSON TWENTY

Objective:
　　To give students time to work on their projects

Activity
　　Give students this class period to work on their projects.

LESSON TWENTY-ONE

Objectives:
　　1. To discuss major themes, ideas and narrative techniques in *Great Expectations*
　　2. To give students the opportunity to practice their group interaction skills

Activity #1
　　Divide your class into seven groups--one group for each of the following topics:
　　　　1. "Wealth is corrupting"
　　　　2. "Goodness comes from self, not money"
　　　　3. "Magwitch, Joe and Pip are victims"
　　　　4. Dickens' use of coincidence
　　　　5. Humor in *Great Expectations*
　　　　6. Law/jail/courts and Dickens' treatment of our justice system
　　　　7. Good Guys and Bad Guys in *Great Expectations*

　　Allow the groups time to find specific examples of their topics in the novel. Allow time for the group members to discuss their findings and come up with some intelligent statements about the topic. The groups should appoint a spokesperson to report the group's thoughts.

Activity #2
　　Ask each group's spokesperson to give the group's thoughts about the topic. Jot these down on the board or overhead projector and use them as a springboard for a discussion of the topics.

LESSON TWENTY-TWO

Objectives:
1. To discuss the major themes in the novel
2. To allow students time to review, compare and correct their notes

Activity #1

Use the groups' work as a nucleus and a springboard for discussions about the major themes in the novel. Call on individual group members by chapter(s) to give the examples they found of their theme in those chapters. Jot them down briefly for students to copy into their notes.

Ask the group spokesperson to give the group's thoughts about the theme development so far. Jot these down.

Ask if anyone from the group has anything to add.

Take the time to discuss each theme thoroughly with the class and be sure to allow time for students (either members of the group or other class members) to express their ideas or ask questions.

NOTE: Having students report in this manner takes a little longer than having just one student from each group report, but it holds all group members accountable for their work.

Activity #2

Allow any remaining time for students to review, compare and/or correct their notes.

LESSON TWENTY-THREE

Objective
 To review the main ideas presented in *Great Expectations*

Activity #1
 Choose one of the review games/activities included in the packet and spend your class period as outlined there. Some materials for these activities are located in the Extra Activities Packet section of this unit.

Activity #2
 Remind students that the Unit Test will be in the next class meeting. Stress the review of the Study Guides and their class notes as a last minute, brush-up review for homework.

REVIEW GAMES/ACTIVITIES - *Great Expectations*

1. Ask the class to make up a unit test for *Great Expectations*. The test should have 4 sections: matching, true/false, short answer, and essay. Students may use 1/2 period to make the test and then swap papers and use the other 1/2 class period to take a test a classmate has devised. (open book). You may want to use the unit test included in this packet or take questions from the students' unit tests to formulate your own test.

2. Take 1/2 period for students to make up true and false questions (including the answers). Collect the papers and divide the class into two teams. Draw a big tic-tac-toe board on the chalk board. Make one team X and one team O. Ask questions to each side, giving each student one turn. If the question is answered correctly, that students' team's letter (X or O) is placed in the box. If the answer is incorrect, no mark is placed in the box. The object is to get three marks in a row like tic-tac-toe. You may want to keep track of the number of games won for each team.

3. Take 1/2 period for students to make up questions (true/false and short answer). Collect the questions. Divide the class into two teams. You'll alternate asking questions to individual members of teams A & B (like in a spelling bee). The question keeps going from A to B until it is correctly answered, then a new question is asked. A correct answer does not allow the team to get another question. Correct answers are +2 points; incorrect answers are -1 point.

4. Have students pair up and quiz each other from their study guides and class notes.

5. Give students a *Great Expectations* crossword puzzle to complete.

6. Divide your class into two teams. Use the *Great Expectations* crossword words with their letters jumbled as a word list. Student 1 from Team A faces off against Student 1 from Team B. You write the first jumbled word on the board. The first student (1A or 1B) to unscramble the word wins the chance for his/her team to score points. If 1A wins the jumble, go to student 2A and give him/her a clue. He/she must give you the correct word which matches that clue. If he/she does, Team A scores a point, and you give student 3A a clue for which you expect another correct response. Continue giving Team A clues until some team member makes an incorrect response. An incorrect response sends the game back to the jumbled-word face off, this time with students 2A and 2B. Instead of repeating giving clues to the first few students of each team, continue with the student after the one who gave the last incorrect response on the team. For example, if Team B wins the jumbled-word face-off, and student 5B gave the last incorrect answer for Team B, you would start this round of clue questions with student 6B, and so on. The team with the most points wins!

UNIT TESTS

SHORT ANSWER UNIT TEST 1 - *Great Expectations*

I. Matching/Identify

___ 1. Magwitch   A. Pip's confidant at the Gargery's

___ 2. Joe   B. "The pale, young gentleman"; Pip's flatmate

___ 3. Jaggers   C. Marries Estella

___ 4. Estella   D. Pip's benefactor

___ 5. Pip   E. Pip's brother-in-law; blacksmith

___ 6. Molly   F. Tries to kill Pip

___ 7. Pumblechook   G. Spinster woman who uses Pip

___ 8. Orlick   H. He has great expectations

___ 9. Wopsle   I. Estella's mother; Jaggers' servant

___ 10. Biddy   J. Miss Havisham's adopted daughter

___ 11. Miss Havisham   K. Wemmick's father

___ 12. Mrs. Joe   L. Pip's servant

___ 13. Herbert   M. Church clerk turned actor

___ 14. Wemmick   N. Pip's sister

___ 15. Drummle   O. Herbert's girlfriend (later wife)

___ 16. Compeyson   P. Enemy of Magwitch; jilted Miss Havisham

___ 17. The Avenger   Q. Claimed to be the founder of Pip's fortunes

___ 18. Clara   R. Jaggers' clerk

___ 19. The Aged P.   S. An attorney; Pip's guardian

___ 20. Startop   T. Helped Pip and Herbert; former roommate at Pockets'

Great Expectations Short Answer Unit Test I Page 2

II. Short Answer

1. Explain how Pip and Joe were "brought up by hand."

2. How does Pip feel about himself after his first meeting with Miss Havisham and Estella?

3. Explain: "Pause you who read this and think for a moment of the long chain of iron or gold, of thorns or flowers, that would never have bound you, but for the formation of the first link on one memorable day."

4. Who claimed to be the founder of Pip's fortunes? Who actually was?

5. What did Pip do for Herbert, and how did his good deed eventually come back to him?

Great Expectations Short Answer Unit Test I Page 3

6. Describe the two sides of Wemmick's character.

7. Why did Orlick try to kill Pip?

8. Pip says, "I only saw him as a much better man than I had been to Joe." Explain how this shows Pip's personal growth.

9. What happened to Pip's "great expectations"?

10. How did Pip carry on with his life?

Great Expectations Short Answer Unit Test I Page 4

III. Composition

What is the point of *Great Expectations*? When we read books, we usually come away from our reading experience a little richer, having given more thought to a particular aspect of life. What do you think Charles Dickens intended us to gain from reading his novel?

Great Expectations Short Answer Unit Test 1 Page 5

IV. Vocabulary

Listen to the vocabulary word and spell it. After you have spelled all the words, go back and write down the definitions.

1.

2.

3.

4.

5.

6.

7.

8.

9.

10.

SHORT ANSWER UNIT TEST 2 - *Great Expectations*

I. Matching

___ 1. Magwitch   A. Miss Havisham's adopted daughter

___ 2. Joe   B. Estella's mother; Jaggers' servant

___ 3. Jaggers   C. He has great expectations

___ 4. Estella   D. Spinster woman who uses Pip

___ 5. Pip   E. Pip's servant

___ 6. Molly   F. Tries to kill Pip

___ 7. Pumblechook   G. Pip's benefactor

___ 8. Orlick   H. Pip's confidant at the Gargery's

___ 9. Wopsle   I. "The pale, young gentleman"; Pip's flatmate

___ 10. Biddy   J. Marries Estella

___ 11. Miss Havisham   K. Wemmick's father

___ 12. Mrs. Joe   L. Herbert's girlfriend (later wife)

___ 13. Herbert   M. Enemy of Magwitch; jilted Miss Havisham

___ 14. Wemmick   N. Pip's sister

___ 15. Drummle   O. Pip's brother-in-law; blacksmith

___ 16. Compeyson   P. An attorney; Pip's guardian

___ 17. The Avenger   Q. Jaggers' clerk

___ 18. Clara   R. Claimed to be the founder of Pip's fortunes

___ 19. The Aged P.   S. Church clerk turned actor

___ 20. Startop   T. Helped Pip and Herbert; former roommate at Pockets'

Great Expectations Short Answer Unit Test 2 page 2

II. Short Answer

1. Explain how Pip and Joe were "brought up by hand."

2. "Pause you who read this, and think for a moment of the long chain of iron or gold, of thorns or flowers, that would never have bound you, but for the formation of the first link on one memorable day." Explain the significance of this quote.

3. Explain "Brag is a good dog, but Holdfast is a better."

4. What is Pip's great expectation?

5. Joe says, "I'm all wrong in these clothes." Explain why.

6. ". . . I thought of the beautiful young Estella . . . with absolute abhorrence of the contrast between the jail and her." Explain why this statement is ironic.

7. Estella says, "I am what you have made me." Explain.

Great Expectations Short Answer Unit Test 2 page 3

8. Explain how Miss Havisham has used Pip.

9. "Don't be afraid of my being a blessing to him, I shall not be that." (Estella to Pip) Explain what Estella means.

10. Pip says, "I only saw him as a much better man than I had been to Joe." Explain how this shows Pip's growth as a character.

11. What happened to Pip's "great expectations"?

Great Expectations Short Answer Unit Test 2 page 4

III. Composition

What were three themes in *Great Expectations*? Write one paragraph about each, giving a full explanation of each and telling how Dickens presented the theme in the novel.

Great Expectations Short Answer Unit Test 2 page 5

IV. Vocabulary
Listen to the vocabulary word and spell it. After you have spelled all the words, go back and write down the definition.

1.

2.

3.

4.

5.

6.

7.

8.

9.

10.

KEY: SHORT ANSWER UNIT TESTS - *Great Expectations*

The short answer questions are taken directly from the study guides.
If you need to look up the answers, you will find them in the study guide section.

Answers to the composition questions will vary depending on your
class discussions and the level of your students.

For the vocabulary section of the test, choose ten of the
words from the vocabulary lists to read orally for your students.

The answers to the matching section of the test are below.

Answers to the matching section of the Advanced Short Answer Unit Test
are the same as for Short Answer Unit Test #2.

<u>Test #1</u>
1. D
2. E
3. S
4. J
5. H
6. I
7. Q
8. F
9. M
10. A
11. G
12. N
13. B
14. R
15. C
16. P
17. L
18. O
19. K
20. T

<u>Test #2</u>
1. G
2. O
3. P
4. A
5. C
6. B
7. R
8. F
9. S
10. H
11. D
12. N
13. I
14. Q
15. J
16. M
17. E
18. L
19. K
20. T

ADVANCED SHORT ANSWER UNIT TEST - *Great Expectations*

I. Matching

___ 1. Magwitch   A. Miss Havisham's adopted daughter

___ 2. Joe   B. Estella's mother; Jaggers' servant

___ 3. Jaggers   C. He has great expectations

___ 4. Estella   D. Spinster woman who uses Pip

___ 5. Pip   E. Pip's servant

___ 6. Molly   F. Tries to kill Pip

___ 7. Pumblechook   G. Pip's benefactor

___ 8. Orlick   H. Pip's confidant at the Gargery's

___ 9. Wopsle   I. "The pale, young gentleman"; Pip's flatmate

___ 10. Biddy   J. Marries Estella

___ 11. Miss Havisham   K. Wemmick's father

___ 12. Mrs. Joe   L. Herbert's girlfriend (later wife)

___ 13. Herbert   M. Enemy of Magwitch; jilted Miss Havisham

___ 14. Wemmick   N. Pip's sister

___ 15. Drummle   O. Pip's brother-in-law; blacksmith

___ 16. Compeyson   P. An attorney; Pip's guardian

___ 17. The Avenger   Q. Jaggers' clerk

___ 18. Clara   R. Claimed to be the founder of Pip's fortunes

___ 19. The Aged P.   S. Church clerk turned actor

___ 20. Startop   T. Helped Pip and Herbert; former roommate at Pockets'

Great Expectations Advanced Short Answer Unit Test page 2

II. Short Answer

1. Describe Pip's relationships with each of the following characters: Joe, Biddy, Mrs. Joe, Miss Havisham, Estella, Magwitch, and Orlick.

2. Discuss ways in which Dickens uses the characters and events in *Great Expectations* to show that wealth is corrupting.

3. "Pause you who read this, and think for a moment of the long chain of iron or gold, of thorns or flowers, that would never have bound you, but for the formation of the first link on one memorable day." Explain the significance of this quote.

Great Expectations Advanced Short Answer Unit Test page 3

4. Pip says, "I only saw him as a much better man than I had been to Joe." Explain how this shows Pip's growth as a character.

5. "Goodness comes from self, not money." Explain using characters, themes and ideas from *Great Expectations*.

6. "Magwitch, Joe and Pip are victims." Explain using characters, themes and ideas from *Great Expectations*.

Great Expectations Advanced Short Answer Unit Test page 4

III. Composition

What was the most important idea Charles Dickens put forth in *Great Expectations*? Use examples from the text to support and justify your answer. This is a <u>composition</u> (<u>not</u> a short answer) question.

Great Expectations Advanced Short Answer Unit Test page 5

IV. Vocabulary

Listen to the vocabulary words and write them down. Go back later and write a composition in which you use all of the vocabulary words. The composition must relate in some way to *Great Expectations*.

MULTIPLE CHOICE UNIT TEST 1 - *Great Expectations*

I. Matching/Identify

___ 1. Magwitch   A. Pip's confidant at the Gargery's

___ 2. Joe   B. "The pale, young gentleman"; Pip's flatmate

___ 3. Jaggers   C. Marries Estella

___ 4. Estella   D. Pip's benefactor

___ 5. Pip   E. Pip's brother-in-law; blacksmith

___ 6. Molly   F. Tries to kill Pip

___ 7. Pumblechook   G. Spinster woman who uses Pip

___ 8. Orlick   H. He has great expectations

___ 9. Wopsle   I. Estella's mother; Jaggers' servant

___ 10. Biddy   J. Miss Havisham's adopted daughter

___ 11. Miss Havisham   K. Wemmick's father

___ 12. Mrs. Joe   L. Pip's servant

___ 13. Herbert   M. Church clerk turned actor

___ 14. Wemmick   N. Pip's sister

___ 15. Drummle   O. Herbert's girlfriend (later wife)

___ 16. Compeyson   P. Enemy of Magwitch; jilted Miss Havisham

___ 17. The Avenger   Q. Claimed to be the founder of Pip's fortunes

___ 18. Clara   R. Jaggers' clerk

___ 19. The Aged P.   S. An attorney; Pip's guardian

___ 20. Startop   T. Helped Pip and Herbert; former roommate at Pockets'

Great Expectations Multiple Choice Unit Test 1 Page 2

II. Multiple Choice

1. Explain how Pip and Joe were "brought up by hand."
    A. Mrs. Joe made all of their food and clothes herself.
    B. Mrs. Joe nursed both of them back to health when they got sick.
    C. Mrs. Joe frequently spanked Pip and threatened Joe.
    D. Mrs. Joe took an active interest in everything Pip and Joe did.

2. "Pause you who read this, and think for a moment of the long chain of iron or gold, of thorns or flowers, that would never have bound you, but for the formation of the first link on one memorable day." Explain the significance of this quote with regard to Pip.
    A. He is falling in love with Estella.
    B. It is his fate to be a blacksmith because his parents are dead and he has to do what his sister wants.
    C. His whole life is changed by meeting the convict.
    D. Miss Havisham has been a bad influence on him.

3. Explain "Brag is a good dog, but Holdfast is better."
    A. Pip's pet is much smarter than Estella's.
    B. It is better to keep your word than to make weak promises.
    C. Brag and Holdfast are two of the dogs used to hunt escaped convicts.
    D. Confidence is good to have, but determination is better.

4. What is Pip's great expectation?
    A. He will become an excellent blacksmith and marry Biddy.
    B. Miss Havisham will employ him and let him live in her home.
    C. Mrs. Joe will die and leave him and Joe in peace.
    D. He will be educated, made a gentleman, and have a benefactor.

5. Explain why Pip said, "If I could have kept him away by paying money, I certainly would have paid money."
    A. Pip has become a snob and is ashamed of his coarse and common roots, especially Joe.
    B. Pip is embarrassed that he has not yet visited Joe. He thinks offering him some money may help ease the embarrassment.
    C. Pip offered Joe money instead of the visit, but Joe was proud and refused it.
    D. Pip wanted to give Joe some money, but his benefactor had said he could not share it.

Great Expectations Multiple Choice Unit Test 1 Page 3

6. Why does Joe call Pip "Sir?"
    A. Joe is angry and is being sarcastic.
    B. Mr. Wopsle told Joe he had to do it.
    C. It is a sign of respect for Pip's new education and social level.
    D. Joe thinks he is too old to be called a childish name like Pip.

7. Joe says, "I'm all wrong in these clothes." Explain why.
    A. Dressing in his Sunday best makes him uncomfortable, and symbolizes his discomfort in a different social class.
    B. He is jealous that Pip's clothes are of a better quality, and hopes that Pip will offer to buy him a new suit.
    C. He has lost weight since Mrs. Joe became ill, but he cannot afford new Sunday clothes. He is afraid Pip will make fun of him.
    D. Pip says he would have liked to have seen Joe in his blacksmith clothes, to remind him of the old days. Joe agrees.

8. What was the subject of the disagreement between Estella and Miss Havisham?
    A. Estella wanted Miss Havisham's jewels, but Miss Havisham did not want to give them to her.
    B. Miss Havisham wants Estella to stay at the house, but Estella wants to go back to France to study. Miss Havisham says she is selfish.
    C. Estella is cold and unfeeling toward Miss Havisham. She thinks Estella is ungrateful, but Estella reminds her that she (Estella) has been raised that way by Miss Havisham.
    D. Miss Havisham wants Estella and Pip to become engaged. Estella says she doesn't want to marry someone with such common roots. Miss Havisham reminds her that she (Estella) also had common roots, and should be grateful to be guaranteed of a husband with money and position.

9. "Don't be afraid of my being a blessing to him, I shall not be that." What does Estella mean when she says that to Pip?
    A. Pip should think only of her and her happiness.
    B. She will marry Drummle, but intends to make him miserable.
    C. Even though she is going to marry another, Pip is still special to her.
    D. She knows she has common roots and will never really be a gentlewoman, even if she marries a gentleman.

Great Expectations Multiple Choice Unit Test 1 Page 4

10. Pip says, "I only saw him as a much better man than I had been to Joe." About whom is he talking, and how does this show Pip's growth as a character?
    A. He sees Wemmick as a model for treating his elders better, because of the way he treats the Aged P.
    B. Mr. Pocket has been much more tolerant of Pip's lack of education than Pip has been of Joe's.
    C. Pip recognizes that Magwitch was a good man even though a convict.
    D. Mr. Jaggers treats Pip better when he loses Estella than Pip treated Joe when Mrs. Joe died.

11. What happened to Pip's 'great expectations?'
    A. Miss Havisham became his new benefactor and his expectations continued.
    B. He was able to keep all of Magwitch's fortune and became a wealthy man.
    C. He used all of Magwitch's money to pay his debts, and went back to the forge to work as a blacksmith.
    D. Magwitch's money and land went to the state, and he realized he would not become a gentleman.

III. Composition

Charles Dickens wrote *Great Expectations* in 1861, and here we are reading it so many years later. Why? What makes this book a "classic"?

Great Expectations Multiple Choice Unit Test 1 Page 5

IV. Vocabulary

___ 1. Loitered   a. At odds; not matching

___ 2. Latent   b. Neighboring; adjacent

___ 3. Obdurate   c. Damaging

___ 4. Prevailing   d. Consented without argument

___ 5. Assiduity   e. Present but not active; hidden

___ 6. Corroborated   f. Carefree & lighthearted

___ 7. Synopsis   g. Totally reject

___ 8. Tithe   h. Full of or showing servile compliance

___ 9. Obsequious   i. Constant personal attention

___ 10. Detrimental   j. State of dread or alarm

___ 11. Incongruity   k. Braided

___ 12. Contiguous   l. Condition of being temporarily set aside

___ 13. Blithe   m. Summary

___ 14. Insolently   n. One tenth

___ 15. Propensities   o. Insultingly; rudely

___ 16. Acquiesced   p. Most common; widespread

___ 17. Abeyance   q. Hard-hearted; not giving in to persuasion

___ 18. Trepidation   r. Tendencies

___ 19. Plaited   s. Dawdled; proceeded slowly or with many stops

___ 20. Repudiate   t. Supported by other evidence

MULTIPLE CHOICE UNIT TEST 2 - *Great Expectations*

I. Matching

___ 1. Magwitch   A. Miss Havisham's adopted daughter

___ 2. Joe   B. Estella's mother; Jaggers' servant

___ 3. Jaggers   C. He has great expectations

___ 4. Estella   D. Spinster woman who uses Pip

___ 5. Pip   E. Pip's servant

___ 6. Molly   F. Tries to kill Pip

___ 7. Pumblechook   G. Pip's benefactor

___ 8. Orlick   H. Pip's confidant at the Gargery's

___ 9. Wopsle   I. "The pale, young gentleman"; Pip's flatmate

___ 10. Biddy   J. Marries Estella

___ 11. Miss Havisham   K. Wemmick's father

___ 12. Mrs. Joe   L. Herbert's girlfriend (later wife)

___ 13. Herbert   M. Enemy of Magwitch; jilted Miss Havisham

___ 14. Wemmick   N. Pip's sister

___ 15. Drummle   O. Pip's brother-in-law; blacksmith

___ 16. Compeyson   P. An attorney; Pip's guardian

___ 17. The Avenger   Q. Jaggers' clerk

___ 18. Clara   R. Claimed to be the founder of Pip's fortunes

___ 19. The Aged P.   S. Church clerk turned actor

___ 20. Startop   T. Helped Pip and Herbert; former roommate at Pockets'

Great Expectations Multiple Choice Unit Test 2 Page 2

II. Multiple Choice
1. Explain how Pip and Joe were "brought up by hand."
    A. Mrs. Joe made all of their food and clothes herself.
    B. Mrs. Joe frequently spanked Pip and threatened Joe.
    C. Mrs. Joe nursed both of them back to health when they got sick.
    D. Mrs. Joe took an active interest in everything Pip and Joe did.

2. "Pause you who read this, and think for a moment of the long chain of iron or gold, of thorns or flowers, that would never have bound you, but for the formation of the first link on one memorable day." Explain the significance of this quote with regard to Pip.
    A. His whole life is changed by meeting the convict.
    B. It is his fate to be a blacksmith because his parents are dead and he has to do what his sister wants.
    C. He is falling in love with Estella.
    D. Miss Havisham has been a bad influence on him.

3. Explain "Brag is a good dog, but Holdfast is a better."
    A. Pip's pet is much smarter than Estella's.
    B. Confidence is good to have, but determination is better.
    C. Brag and Holdfast are two of the dogs used to hunt escaped convicts.
    D. It is better to keep your word than to make weak promises.

4. What is Pip's great expectation?
    A. He will become an excellent blacksmith and marry Biddy.
    B. Miss Havisham will employ him and let him live in her home.
    C. He will be educated, made a gentleman, and have a benefactor.
    D. Mrs. Joe will die and leave him and Joe in peace.

5. Explain why Pip said, "If I could have kept him away by paying money, I certainly would have paid money."
    A. Pip wanted to give Joe some money, but his benefactor had said he could not share it.
    B. Pip is embarrassed that he has not yet visited Joe. He thinks offering him some money may help ease the embarrassment.
    C. Pip offered Joe money instead of the visit, but Joe was proud and refused it.
    D. Pip has become a snob and is ashamed of his coarse and common roots, especially Joe.

Great Expectations Multiple Choice Unit Test 2 Page 3

6. Why does Joe call Pip "Sir?"
    A. Joe is angry and is being sarcastic.
    B. Mr. Wopsle told Joe he had to do it.
    C. Joe thinks he is too old to be called a childish name like Pip.
    D. It is a sign of respect for Pip's new education and social level.

7. Joe says, "I'm all wrong in these clothes." Explain why.
    A. He is jealous that Pip's clothes are of a better quality, and hopes that Pip will offer to buy him a new suit.
    B. Dressing in his Sunday best makes him uncomfortable, and symbolizes his discomfort in a different social class.
    C. He has lost weight since Mrs. Joe became ill, but he cannot afford new Sunday clothes. He is afraid Pip will make fun of him.
    D. Pip says he would have liked to have seen Joe in his blacksmith clothes, to remind him of the old days. Joe agrees.

8. What was the subject of the disagreement between Estella and Miss Havisham?
    A. Estella is cold and unfeeling toward Miss Havisham. She thinks Estella is ungrateful, but Estella reminds her that she (Estella) has been raised that way by Miss Havisham.
    B. Miss Havisham wants Estella to stay at the house, but Estella wants to go back to France to study. Miss Havisham says she is selfish.
    C. Estella wanted Miss Havisham's jewels, but Miss Havisham did not want to give them to her.
    D. Miss Havisham wants Estella and Pip to become engaged. Estella says she doesn't want to marry someone with such common roots. Miss Havisham reminds her that she (Estella) also had common roots, and should be grateful to be guaranteed of a husband with money and position.

9. "Don't be afraid of my being a blessing to him, I shall not be that." What does Estella mean when she says that to Pip?
    A. Pip should think only of her and her happiness.
    B. Even though she is going to marry another, Pip is still special to her.
    C. She will marry Drummle, but intends to make him miserable.
    D. She knows she has common roots and will never really be a gentlewoman, even if she marries a gentleman.

Great Expectations Multiple Choice Unit Test 2 Page 4

10. Pip says, "I only saw him as a much better man than I had been to Joe." About whom is he talking, and how does this show Pip's growth as a character?
    A. He sees Wemmick as a model for treating his elders better, because of the way he treats the Aged P.
    B. Pip recognizes that Magwitch was a good man even though a convict.
    C. Mr. Pocket has been much more tolerant of Pip's lack of education than Pip has been of Joe's.
    D. Mr. Jaggers treats Pip better when he loses Estella than Pip treated Joe when Mrs. Joe died.

11. What happened to Pip's 'great expectations?'
    A. Magwitch's money and land went to the state, and he realized he would not become a gentleman.
    B. He was able to keep all of Magwitch's fortune and became a wealthy man.
    C. He used all of Magwitch's money to pay his debts, and went back to the forge to work as a blacksmith.
    D. Miss Havisham became his new benefactor and his expectations continued.

III. Composition

Charles Dickens wrote *Great Expectations* in 1861 in England, about the time of the American Civil War. He died in 1870, but suppose you could travel back in time and talk to him about what many people consider his best novel, *Great Expectations*. What would you tell him and/or ask him? Remember, this is an <u>essay</u> question, not a short answer. Be specific and complete, and show off as much knowledge of the book as you can.

Great Expectations Multiple Choice Unit Test 2 Page 5

IV. Vocabulary:

___ 1. ABEYANCE   A. By accident or chance

___ 2. REFECTORIES   B. Sense that something is about to happen

___ 3. PROPENSITIES   C. Faithfulness; loyalty

___ 4. PRESENTIMENT   D. Fever & chills

___ 5. SYNOPSIS   E. Distinct; forceful, effective & vigorous

___ 6. LATENT   F. Condition of being temporarily set aside

___ 7. FORTUITOUSLY   G. Pleased; willing; obliged

___ 8. UNSCRUPULOUS   H. Lacking reverence, respect or dutifulness

___ 9. FIDELITY   I. Summary

___ 10. FAIN   J. Rooms where meals are served

___ 11. AGUE   K. Looked over with care

___ 12. IMPETUOSITY   L. Tendencies

___ 13. TRENCHANT   M. Release from an entanglement

___ 14. AUGMENTED   N. Present but not active; hidden

___ 15. IMPIOUSLY   O. Forcefully; passionately

___ 16. PERUSED   P. Belittling

___ 17. AUSPICIOUS   Q. Added to

___ 18. EXTRICATE   R. Without a conscience or a moral code

___ 19. DEPRECIATION   S. Marked by success; grand

___ 20. MALIGNANT   T. Disposed towards evil

ANSWER SHEET - *Great Expectations*
Multiple Choice Unit Tests

I. Matching	II. Multiple Choice	IV. Vocabulary
1. ___	1. ___	1. ___
2. ___	2. ___	2. ___
3. ___	3. ___	3. ___
4. ___	4. ___	4. ___
5. ___	5. ___	5. ___
6. ___	6. ___	6. ___
7. ___	7. ___	7. ___
8. ___	8. ___	8. ___
9. ___	9. ___	9. ___
10. ___	10. ___	10. ___
11. ___	11. ___	11. ___
12. ___	12. ___	12. ___
13. ___	13. ___	13. ___
14. ___	14. ___	14. ___
15. ___		15. ___
16. ___		16. ___
17. ___		17. ___
		18. ___
		19. ___
		20. ___

ANSWER KEY - *Great Expectations*
Multiple Choice Unit Tests

Answers to Unit Test 1 are in the left column. Answers to Unit Test 2 are in the right column.

I. Matching		II. Multiple Choice		IV. Vocabulary	
1. D	G	1. C	B	1. S	F
2. E	O	2. C	A	2. E	J
3. S	P	3. D	B	3. Q	L
4. J	A	4. D	C	4. P	B
5. H	C	5. A	D	5. I	I
6. I	B	6. C	D	6. T	N
7. Q	R	7. A	B	7. M	A
8. F	F	8. C	A	8. N	R
9. M	S	9. B	C	9. H	C
10. A	H	10. C	B	10. C	G
11. G	D	11. D	A	11. A	D
12. N	N			12. B	O
13. B	I			13. F	E
14. R	Q			14. O	Q
15. C	J			15. R	H
16. P	M			16. D	K
17. L	E			17. L	S
18. O	L			18. J	M
19. K	K			19. K	P
20. T	T			20. G	T

UNIT RESOURCE MATERIALS

BULLETIN BOARD IDEAS - *Great Expectations*

1. Save one corner of the board for the best of students' *Great Expectations* writing assignments.

2. Take one of the word search puzzles from the extra activities packet and with a marker copy it over in a large size on the bulletin board. Write the clue words to find to one side. Invite students prior to and after class to find the words and circle them on the bulletin board. Cut out letters to title the board, " SEARCHING FOR GREAT EXPECTATIONS."

3. Write several of the most significant quotations from the book onto the board on brightly colored paper.

4. Make a bulletin board listing the vocabulary words for this unit. As you complete sections of the novel and discuss the vocabulary for each section, write the definitions on the bulletin board. (If your board is one students face frequently, it will help them learn the words.)

5. Title the board "EVERYONE HAS GREAT EXPECTATIONS." On colorful paper post pictures of things people would hope to do or be -- things people would have as "great expectations." Along the same lines, you could have students bring in pictures (or anything that could be stapled to the board!) that represent their great expectations.

6. Title the board "CHARLES DICKENS (1812-1870)." In the center of the board, post an article summarizing his life. Around that, staple up book jackets or cut-out "books" (from construction paper) with the titles of his most famous works showing. You may wish to write names of some of his most memorable characters from these works near or in the appropriate "book."

7. Title the board, "GETTING A JOB." Make an enlarged version of the Sample Resume' and post it on the board. Also make a copy of the FINDING A JOB tips and post that on the board.

8. Make a bulletin board about different career opportunities.
    a. Get materials from your school's guidance/career placement office and post them on the board.
    b. When your class brainstorms ideas of different occupations, write them up on the bulletin board--or let the students go to the board and write their own ideas.
    c. Go to your school's guidance/career placement office and get a list of occupations. Put up white background paper on your bulletin board. Use different colored markers to write the names of different occupations on the board in columns and rows.

9. Make a bulletin board about financial planning. Perhaps your guest speaker could offer some materials for this one. If not, consider your local banks as sources of information.

EXTRA ACTIVITIES

One of the difficulties in teaching a novel is that all students don't read at the same speed. One student who likes to read may take the book home and finish it in a day or two. Sometimes a few students finish the in-class assignments early. The problem, then, is finding suitable extra activities for students.

The best thing I've found is to keep a little library in the classroom. For this unit on *Great Expectations*, you might check out from the school library other related books and articles about life in London in the 1800's, apprenticeships or schools of higher education, information about salaries for various careers, printed interviews with successful people, or criticisms of Dickens' works. A biography of Dickens or some of his other works might be interesting to some of your students.

Other things you may keep on hand are puzzles. We have made some relating directly to *Great Expectations* for you. Feel free to duplicate them.

Some students may like to draw. You might devise a contest or allow some extra-credit grade for students who draw characters or scenes from *Great Expectations*. Note, too, that if the students do not want to keep their drawings you may pick up some extra bulletin board materials this way. If you have a contest and you supply the prize (a record album or something like that perhaps), you could, possibly, make the drawing itself a non-refundable entry fee.

The pages which follow contain games, puzzles and worksheets. The keys, when appropriate, immediately follow the puzzle or worksheet. There are two main groups of activities: one group for the unit; that is, generally relating to the *Great Expectations* text, and another group of activities related strictly to the *Great Expectations* vocabulary.

Directions for these games, puzzles and worksheets are self-explanatory. The object here is to provide you with extra materials you may use in any way you choose.

MORE ACTIVITIES - *Great Expectations*

1. Pick a chapter or scene with a great deal of dialogue and have the students act it out on a stage. (Perhaps you could assign various scenes to different groups of students so more than one scene could be acted and more students could participate.)

2. Use some of the related topics (noted earlier for an in-class library) as topics for research, reports, written papers, or as topics for guest speakers.

3. Show a film version of *Great Expectations* after you have completed reading the novel in class. Have students evaluate the movie and compare/contrast it with the book. If the students have tried writing a chapter into a scene in a play, you may wish to discuss how the problems they encountered in changing the form were handled in the movie.

4. Have students design a book cover (front and back and inside flaps) for *Great Expectations*.

5. Have students design a bulletin board (ready to be put up; not just sketched) for *Great Expectations.*

6. Take short scenes from the novel. Assign parts in the scenes to various students (so each student has a part). Students should memorize their lines and dress up as their characters to perform their scenes in front of the class in your classroom or on stage.

7. Have students choose one chapter of the novel (with sufficient dialogue) to rewrite as a play. In conjunction with this assignment, have students write a composition explaining the difficulties they encountered in changing from one written form to another.

8. Have students tell Pip's story in a different form: a play, as already noted, or a ballad, a rap song, a poem, etc.

9. Set up a Job Fair in which you invite local businesses to come to your school to explain the kinds of jobs that are available in your area and to show students what they would have to do to get those jobs.

10. Set up an Education Fair in which you invite colleges, trade schools, and corporations with training programs to come to your school in person or to send materials your students could pick up and take home.

11. Have your students plan/set up/carry out 8 and/or 9 above for your school. Students would have to call and/or write to the various businesses/schools, make all the necessary arrangements, and host the event(s).

Great Expectations Word Search

```
C B I D D Y B G R E A T L K D D S H E
L Q N B F C B G G P G N N X Q V E A X
O P I P I G A Z O K C G D Y Z S L V P
T Z Q H K R R R W V J Z R Y T M S I E
H E R B E R T G R A V E Y A R D P S C
E P Z A D E P H L C G Y R V V D T O H T
S V E R R O X J D R C T L K E Y W H A
F I K G U J L N A A O L K G A R B M A T
P W C E M Y R G L P Y C A P F M B H I
F D I M M Q M L F Q I D X R G X V M O
K I L E Q E G K M H S J M A J R B N N
J M R N E T S X M C O M P E Y S O N S
S C O E S R M E T C Q O H B J I A J N
L S P E E J W I M X S F G O N V V X E
J P C G P W W P V I D T E Y F O E T K
P S G T Q G X N T D R J L Z Q R N U C
B A S X A F T I N W S L J Y K P G T I
J K N M V F O A D V O C B F J F E O D
L O N D O N H H X M J O L L Y Y R R T
```

AGEDP	DRUMMLE	HERBERT	PIP
AVENGER	ESTELLA	JAGGERS	PORTER
BARGEMEN	EXPECTATIONS	JOE	POSITION
BIDDY	FIRE	JOLLY	PROVIS
BIRTHDAY	GARGERY	LONDON	STARTOP
BRAG	GRAVEYARD	MAGWITCH	TRABB
CLARA	GRAVY	MOLLY	TUTOR
CLOTHES	GREAT	MRSJOE	WEMMICK
COMPEYSON	HAND	ORLICK	WOPSLE
DICKENS	HAVISHAM	PIE	

Great Expectations Word Search Answer Key

AGEDP	DRUMMLE	HERBERT	PIP
AVENGER	ESTELLA	JAGGERS	PORTER
BARGEMEN	EXPECTATIONS	JOE	POSITION
BIDDY	FIRE	JOLLY	PROVIS
BIRTHDAY	GARGERY	LONDON	STARTOP
BRAG	GRAVEYARD	MAGWITCH	TRABB
CLARA	GRAVY	MOLLY	TUTOR
CLOTHES	GREAT	MRSJOE	WEMMICK
COMPEYSON	HAND	ORLICK	WOPSLE
DICKENS	HAVISHAM	PIE	

Great Expectations Crossword

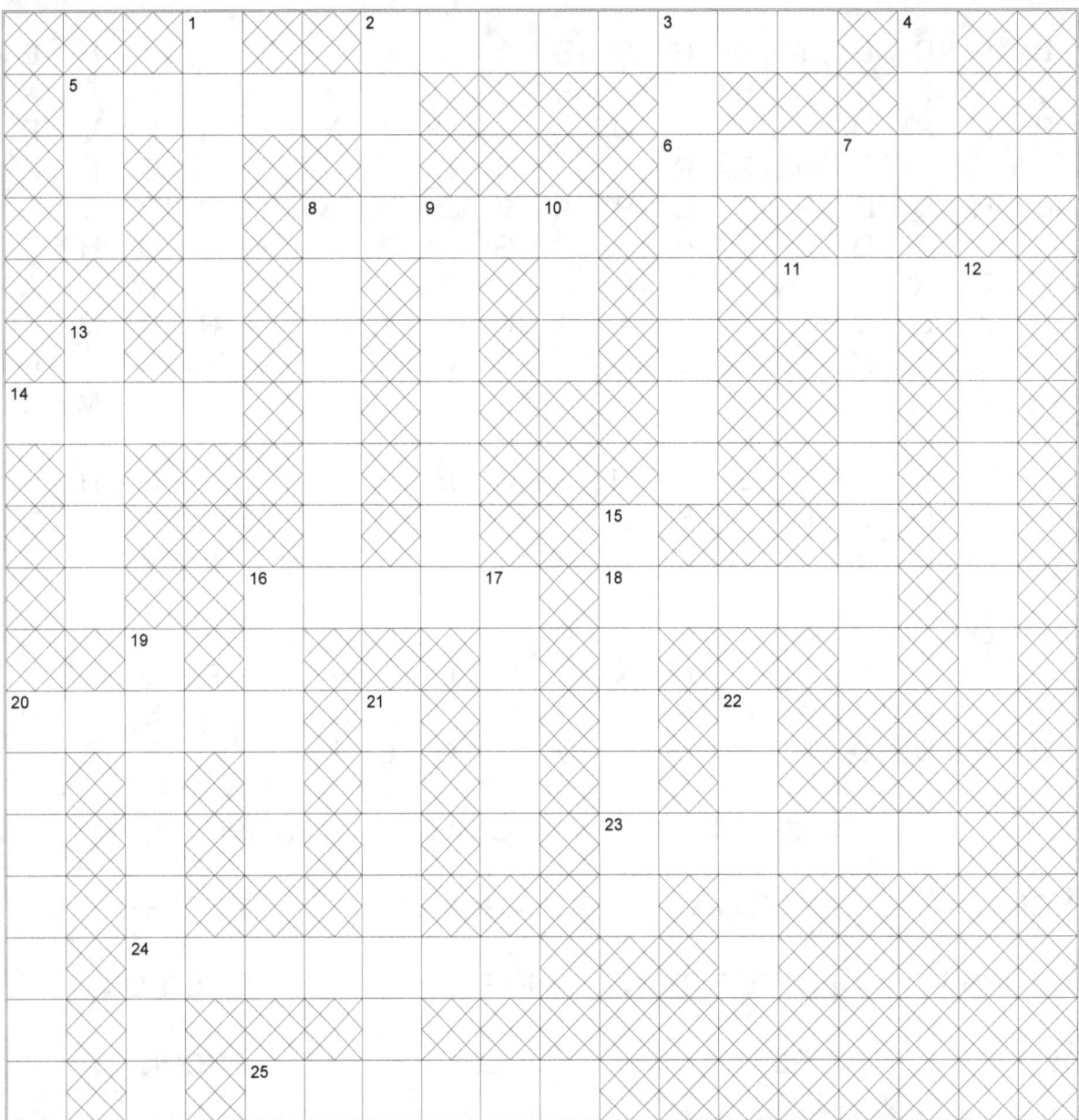

Across
2. Three Jolly____
5. Orlick's position at Miss H's house
6. Joe's last name
8. Wemmick's father
11. Pip and Joe were Brought up by____
14. It burned Miss H and Pip
16. ____Expectations
18. Matthew Pocket to Pip; educator
20. Herbert's girlfriend, later his wife
23. Tries to kill Pip
24. The pale young gentleman; Pip's flatmate
25. Pip's sister

Down
1. Marries Estella
2. ____is a good dog, but Holdfast is a better.
3. Pip's benefactor
4. Pip's blacksmith brother-in-law
5. Pip took pork____to give to the convict
7. Pip meets a convict there
8. Pip's servant
9. Miss Havisham's adopted daughter
10. He has great expectations
12. Author
13. Pip's confidant at the Gargery's
15. Helped Pip and Herbert; former roommate
16. Joe gives Pip extra____at dinner with Mr. P
17. The letter form____& Col brought news of Mrs. Joe's death
19. Spinster woman who uses Pip
20. I'm all wrong in these_____. (Joe said to Pip)
21. Pip's guardian
22. Three_____Bargemen

Great Expectations Crossword Answer Key

Across
2. Three Jolly ____
5. Orlick's position at Miss H's house
6. Joe's last name
8. Wemmick's father
11. Pip and Joe were Brought up by ____
14. It burned Miss H and Pip
16. ____ Expectations
18. Matthew Pocket to Pip; educator
20. Herbert's girlfriend, later his wife
23. Tries to kill Pip
24. The pale young gentleman; Pip's flatmate
25. Pip's sister

Down
1. Marries Estella
2. ____ is a good dog, but Holdfast is a better.
3. Pip's benefactor
4. Pip's blacksmith brother-in-law
5. Pip took pork ____ to give to the convict
7. Pip meets a convict there
8. Pip's servant
9. Miss Havisham's adopted daughter
10. He has great expectations
12. Author
13. Pip's confidant at the Gargery's
15. Helped Pip and Herbert; former roommate
16. Joe gives Pip extra ____ at dinner with Mr. P
17. The letter form ____ & Col brought news of Mrs. Joe's death
19. Spinster woman who uses Pip
20. I'm all wrong in these ____. (Joe said to Pip)
21. Pip's guardian
22. Three ____ Bargemen

MATCHING QUIZ/WORKSHEET 1 - *Great Expectations*

___ 1. FIRE   A. Author

___ 2. BARGEMEN   B. The letter from ___ & Co. brought news of Mrs. Joe's death

___ 3. JOLLY   C. Three Jolly _____

___ 4. GRAVY   D. 'I'm all wrong in these ____.' (Joe said to Pip)

___ 5. CLOTHES   E. It burned Miss H and Pip

___ 6. DICKENS   F. Pip and Joe were 'Brought up by ____'

___ 7. ORLICK   G. Joe gives Pip extra ___ at dinner with Mr. P

___ 8. PIP   H. Great _____

___ 9. EXPECTATIONS   I. Three _____ Bargemen

___ 10. HAND   J. Magwitch's assumed name

___ 11. AVENGER   K. Pip's servant

___ 12. CLARA   L. Pip's sister

___ 13. PROVIS   M. Joe's last name

___ 14. LONDON   N. Tries to kill Pip

___ 15. TRABB   O. Miss Havisham's adopted daughter

___ 16. MRSJOE   P. Jaggers' office is in this city

___ 17. GARGERY   Q. He has great expectations

___ 18. ESTELLA   R. Herbert's girlfriend, later his wife

___ 19. MAGWITCH   S. '_____ is a good dog, but Holdfast is a better.'

___ 20. BRAG   T. Pip's benefactor

KEY: MATCHING QUIZ/WORKSHEET 1 - *Great Expectations*

_E_	1. FIRE	A. Author
_C_	2. BARGEMEN	B. The letter from ___ & Co. brought news of Mrs. Joe's death
_I_	3. JOLLY	C. Three Jolly _____
_G_	4. GRAVY	D. 'I'm all wrong in these ____.' (Joe said to Pip)
_D_	5. CLOTHES	E. It burned Miss H and Pip
_A_	6. DICKENS	F. Pip and Joe were 'Brought up by ____'
_N_	7. ORLICK	G. Joe gives Pip extra ___ at dinner with Mr. P
_Q_	8. PIP	H. Great _____
_H_	9. EXPECTATIONS	I. Three _____ Bargemen
_F_	10. HAND	J. Magwitch's assumed name
_K_	11. AVENGER	K. Pip's servant
_R_	12. CLARA	L. Pip's sister
_J_	13. PROVIS	M. Joe's last name
_P_	14. LONDON	N. Tries to kill Pip
_B_	15. TRABB	O. Miss Havisham's adopted daughter
_L_	16. MRSJOE	P. Jaggers' office is in this city
_M_	17. GARGERY	Q. He has great expectations
_O_	18. ESTELLA	R. Herbert's girlfriend, later his wife
_T_	19. MAGWITCH	S. '_____ is a good dog, but Holdfast is a better.'
_S_	20. BRAG	T. Pip's benefactor

MATCHING QUIZ/WORKSHEET 2 - *Great Expectations*

___ 1. PIP A. Wemmick's father

___ 2. JOE B. Helped Pip and Herbert; for roommate

___ 3. HERBERT C. Pip's blacksmith brother-in-law

___ 4. BRAG D. Pip's sister

___ 5. PROVIS E. Orlick's position at Miss H's house

___ 6. CLOTHES F. Joe's last name

___ 7. GARGERY G. Author

___ 8. PIE H. The letter from ___ & Co. brought news of Mrs. Joe's death

___ 9. TRABB I. 'I'm all wrong in these ____.' (Joe said to Pip)

___ 10. PORTER J. The 'pale young gentleman'; Pip's flatmate

___ 11. EXPECTATIONS K. He has great expectations

___ 12. STARTOP L. Great _____

___ 13. MRSJOE M. Claimed to be the founder of Pip's fortunes

___ 14. CLARA N. Pip took pork ___ to give to the convict

___ 15. PUMBLECHOOK O. '____ is a good dog, but Holdfast is a better.'

___ 16. GRAVY P. Church clerk turned actor

___ 17. AGEDP Q. Magwitch's assumed name

___ 18. WOPSLE R. Herbert's girlfriend, later his wife

___ 19. MOLLY S. Estella's mother; Jaggers' servant

___ 20. DICKENS T. Joe gives Pip extra ___ at dinner with Mr. P

KEY: MATCHING QUIZ/WORKSHEET 2 - *Great Expectations*

K	1. PIP	A. Wemmick's father
C	2. JOE	B. Helped Pip and Herbert; for roommate
J	3. HERBERT	C. Pip's blacksmith brother-in-law
O	4. BRAG	D. Pip's sister
Q	5. PROVIS	E. Orlick's position at Miss H's house
I	6. CLOTHES	F. Joe's last name
F	7. GARGERY	G. Author
N	8. PIE	H. The letter from ___ & Co. brought news of Mrs. Joe's death
H	9. TRABB	I. 'I'm all wrong in these ___.' (Joe said to Pip)
E	10. PORTER	J. The 'pale young gentleman'; Pip's flatmate
L	11. EXPECTATIONS	K. He has great expectations
B	12. STARTOP	L. Great _____
D	13. MRSJOE	M. Claimed to be the founder of Pip's fortunes
R	14. CLARA	N. Pip took pork ___ to give to the convict
M	15. PUMBLECHOOK	O. '_____ is a good dog, but Holdfast is a better.'
T	16. GRAVY	P. Church clerk turned actor
A	17. AGEDP	Q. Magwitch's assumed name
P	18. WOPSLE	R. Herbert's girlfriend, later his wife
S	19. MOLLY	S. Estella's mother; Jaggers' servant
G	20. DICKENS	T. Joe gives Pip extra ___ at dinner with Mr. P

JUGGLE LETTER REVIEW GAME CLUE SHEET - *Great Expectations*

SCRAMBLED	WORD	CLUE
PPI	PIP	He has great expectations
ASAHMVIH	HAVISHAM	Spinster woman who uses Pip
NNOLDO	LONDON	Jagger's office is in this city
IYDDB	BIDDY	Pip's confidant at the Gargery's
RAGB	BRAG	'_____ is a good dog, but Holdfast is a better."
OIRSVP	PROVIS	Magwitch's assumed name
EJO	JOE	Pip's blacksmith brother-in-law
RAVYG	GRAVY	Joe gives Pip extra _____ at dinner with Mr. P.
NEREAGV	AVENGER	Pip's servant
LEWPOS	WOPSLE	Church clerk turned actor
RVYDAEGAR	GRAVEYARD	Pip meets a convict there
CPEXASEINTTO	EXPECTATIONS	Great _____
IAYHBTRD	BIRTHDAY	Camilla, Raymond & Sara visit Miss H on this day every year
RGEJSAG	JAGGERS	Pip's guardian
KCNIDSE	DICKENS	Author
LEASELT	ESTELLA	Miss Havisham's adopted daughter
IEP	PIE	Pip took pork ____ to give to the convict
DEAPG	AGEDP	Wemmick's father
GNBERAMA	BARGEMAN	Three Jolly _____
YLJOL	JOLLY	Three _____ Bargemen
IKCEMWM	WEMMICK	Jaggers' Clerk
IOPIONST	POSITION	Pip bought one for Herbert so he would have a steady income
ROUTT	TUTOR	Mathew Pocket to Pip; educator
IMTSHLKCAB	BLACKSMITH	Joe's occupation
TRBEREH	HERBERT	The 'pale young gentleman'; Pip's flatmate
IREF	FIRE	It burned Miss H and Pip
LRACA	CLARA	Herbert's girlfriend, later his wife
KCIORL	ORLICK	Tries to kill Pip
ELDMRUM	DRUMMLE	Marries Estella
AOPTSRT	STARTOP	Helped Pip and Herbert, former roommate
AIMCHGWT	MAGWITCH	Pip's benefactor
EYPOSNCOM	COMPEYSON	Enemy of Magwitch; jilted Miss H
GREAGYR	GARGERY	Joe's last name
ABTRB	TRABB	The letter from _____ & Co. brought news of Mrs. Joe's death

VOCABULARY RESOURCE MATERIALS

Great Expectations Vocabulary Word Search

```
P R O P E N S I T I E S O R O M E S K
L L F E L I C I T O U S Y T C C T Y Z
F C A L L U D E D O G B N E N N O N S
E H T I L B D T I T A A R A A D B O W
K C X R T I C C H G H U Y N E K S P X
J R H Y C E I H H C N E G S V U T S N
G D C U J R D D N E B I U U P N I I O
Y W L B A S K E T A L R M E R S N S I
L A A V C K R T T A E A R S D E A E T
T P A I X T K R M P G C M O E I T X A
N P N U M N K O Y N I K T P R R E H D
E R T T S P D S A L F X L E E O L O I
L O T J P P I N I R H U N D T T Y R P
O B S E Q U I O U S E X T R I C A T E
S A K F V M U C U M D T R I O E D E R
N T A S O S Z O I S K H I V L F H D T
I I X U L F I N S O L E N T N E T A L
N O S Y W D Y H G P U Y N B H R C J H
Q N S U O L U P U R C S N U X E S S Y
```

ABEYANCE	DEPOSE	LOITERED	PROPENSITIES
ABJECT	EXHORTED	LUCID	REFECTORIES
AGUE	EXTRICATE	MAGNANIMOUS	SUPERCILIOUSLY
ALLUDED	FAIN	MALIGNANT	SYNOPSIS
APPROBATION	FELICITOUS	MOROSE	TENURE
AUGUR	FUTILE	OBSEQUIOUS	TITHE
AUSPICIOUS	IMPIOUSLY	OBSTINATELY	TRENCHANT
AVARICIOUS	INSOLENT	ODIOUS	TREPIDATION
BLITHE	INSOLENTLY	PERUSED	UNSCRUPULOUS
CONSORTED	LATENT	PLAITED	

Great Expectations Vocabulary Word Search Answer Key

ABEYANCE	DEPOSE	LOITERED	PROPENSITIES
ABJECT	EXHORTED	LUCID	REFECTORIES
AGUE	EXTRICATE	MAGNANIMOUS	SUPERCILIOUSLY
ALLUDED	FAIN	MALIGNANT	SYNOPSIS
APPROBATION	FELICITOUS	MOROSE	TENURE
AUGUR	FUTILE	OBSEQUIOUS	TITHE
AUSPICIOUS	IMPIOUSLY	OBSTINATELY	TRENCHANT
AVARICIOUS	INSOLENT	ODIOUS	TREPIDATION
BLITHE	INSOLENTLY	PERUSED	UNSCRUPULOUS
CONSORTED	LATENT	PLAITED	

Great Expectations Vocabulary Crossword

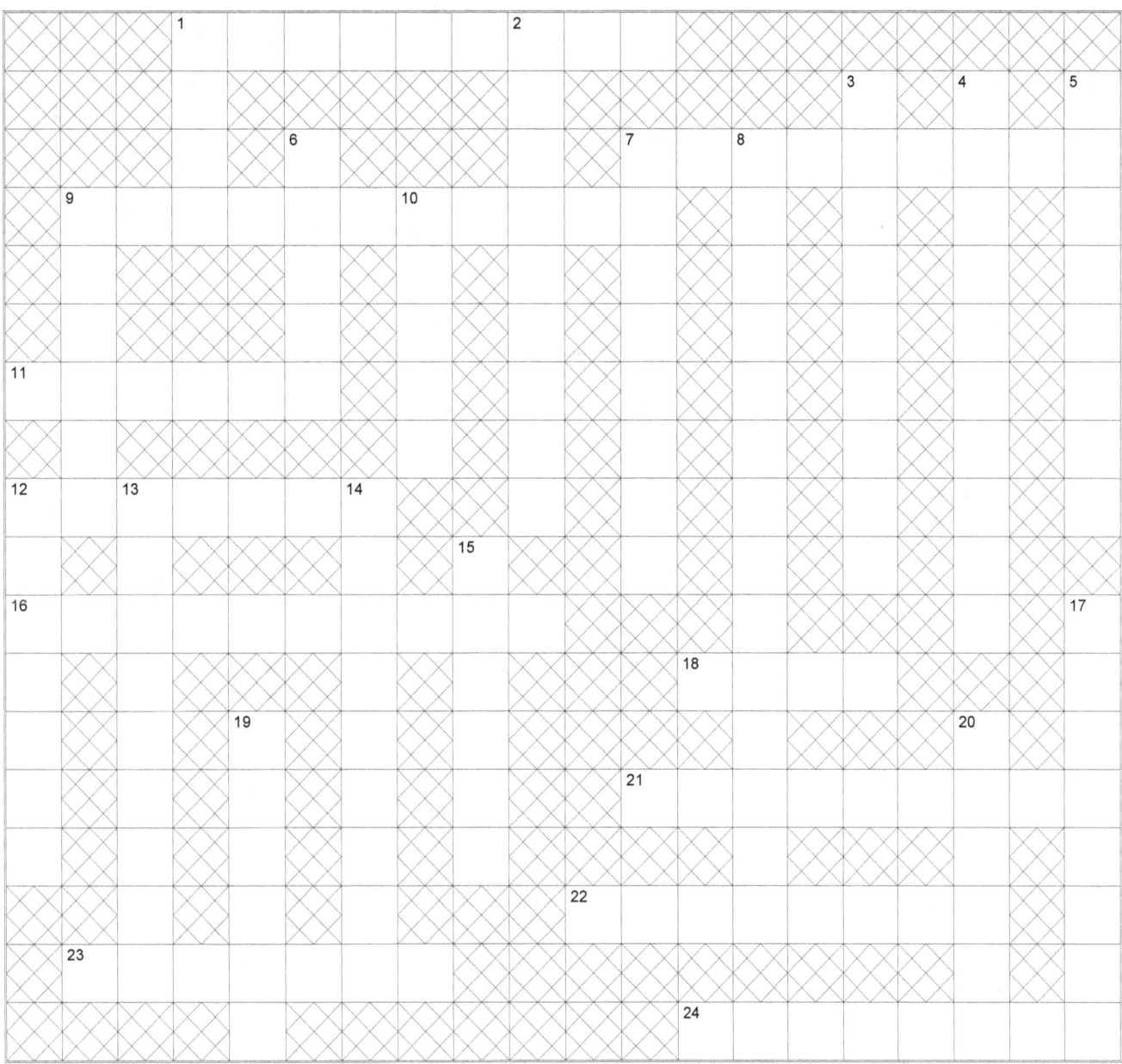

Across
1. Constant personal attention
7. Permanent
9. State of dread or alarm
11. Having no useful result
12. Be present throughout
16. Ghost
18. Pleased; willing; obliged
21. Distinct; forceful, effective & vigorous
22. Condition of being temporarily set aside
23. Looked over with care
24. Urged; advised

Down
1. Fever & chills
2. Lacking reverence, respect or dutifulness
3. Bringing out; drawing forth
4. Full of or showing servile compliance
5. Reserved
6. One tenth
7. Arrogant; insulting
8. Gloomily
9. Period during which something is held
10. Predict
12. Braided
13. Totally reject
14. Release from an entanglement
15. Melancholy; gloomy
17. Dawdled; proceeded slowly or with many stops
19. Arousing strong dislike
20. Present but not active; hidden

Great Expectations Vocabulary Crossword Answer Key

Across
1. Constant personal attention
7. Permanent
9. State of dread or alarm
11. Having no useful result
12. Be present throughout
16. Ghost
18. Pleased; willing; obliged
21. Distinct; forceful, effective & vigorous
22. Condition of being temporarily set aside
23. Looked over with care
24. Urged; advised

Down
1. Fever & chills
2. Lacking reverence, respect or dutifulness
3. Bringing out; drawing forth
4. Full of or showing servile compliance
5. Reserved
6. One tenth
7. Arrogant; insulting
8. Gloomily
9. Period during which something is held
10. Predict
12. Braided
13. Totally reject
14. Release from an entanglement
15. Melancholy; gloomy
17. Dawdled; proceeded slowly or with many stops
19. Arousing strong dislike
20. Present but not active; hidden

VOCABULARY WORKSHEET 1 - *Great Expectations*

___ 1. Predict
    a. Augur   b. Expatriated   c. Consigned   d. Reticent

___ 2. Added to
    a. Repudiate   b. Indelible   c. Augmented   d. Expatriated

___ 3. Whimsical
    a. Detrimental   b. Omnipotent   c. Capricious   d. Depreciation

___ 4. Damaging
    a. Synopsis   b. Malignant   c. Detrimental   d. Execrated

___ 5. Complexities
    a. Depreciation   b. Intricacies   c. Obdurate   d. Unscrupulous

___ 6. Looked over with care
    a. Assiduity   b. Augmented   c. Obsequious   d. Perused

___ 7. Release from an entanglement
    a. Impiously   b. Extricate   c. Corroborated   d. Augmented

___ 8. Lucky
    a. Presentiment   b. Benevolent   c. Felicitous   d. Repudiate

___ 9. Relating to marriage
    a. Connubial   b. Benevolent   c. Corroborated   d. Repudiate

___ 10. Most common; widespread
    a. Repudiate   b. Irresolute   c. Prevailing   d. Benevolent

___ 11. Fever & chills
    a. Abject   b. Tithe   c. Imperiously   d. Ague

___ 12. Destructive; deadly
    a. Execrating   b. Pernicious   c. Blithe   d. Corroborated

___ 13. Melancholy; gloomy
    a. Morose   b. Depreciation   c. Blithe   d. Augur

___ 14. Ghost
    a. Ignominiously   b. Alienate   c. Apparition   d. Blithe

___ 15. Gloomily
    a. Fain   b. Consigned   c. Disconsolately   d. Obsequious

___ 16. Lacking reverence, respect or dutifulness
    a. Ague   b. Incongruity   c. Execrating   d. Impiously

___ 17. Domineeringly; overbearingly
    a. Felicitous   b. Imperiously   c. Epistle   d. Intricacies

___ 18. By accident or chance
    a. Approbation   b. Presentiment   c. Connubial   d. Fortuitously

___ 19. Make a statement of facts
    a. Futile   b. Truculent   c. Felicitous   d. Depose

___ 20. Denounced
    a. Detrimental   b. Asunder   c. Felicitous   d. Execrated

KEY: VOCABULARY WORKSHEET 1 - *Great Expectations*

__A__ 1. Predict
   a. Augur   b. Expatriated   c. Consigned   d. Reticent

__C__ 2. Added to
   a. Repudiate   b. Indelible   c. Augmented   d. Expatriated

__C__ 3. Whimsical
   a. Detrimental   b. Omnipotent   c. Capricious   d. Depreciation

__C__ 4. Damaging
   a. Synopsis   b. Malignant   c. Detrimental   d. Execrated

__C__ 5. Complexities
   a. Depreciation   b. Intricacies   c. Obdurate   d. Unscrupulous

__D__ 6. Looked over with care
   a. Assiduity   b. Augmented   c. Obsequious   d. Perused

__B__ 7. Release from an entanglement
   a. Impiously   b. Extricate   c. Corroborated   d. Augmented

__C__ 8. Lucky
   a. Presentiment   b. Benevolent   c. Felicitous   d. Repudiate

__A__ 9. Relating to marriage
   a. Connubial   b. Benevolent   c. Corroborated   d. Repudiate

__C__ 10. Most common; widespread
   a. Repudiate   b. Irresolute   c. Prevailing   d. Benevolent

__D__ 11. Fever & chills
   a. Abject   b. Tithe   c. Imperiously   d. Ague

__B__ 12. Destructive; deadly
   a. Execrating   b. Pernicious   c. Blithe   d. Corroborated

__A__ 13. Melancholy; gloomy
   a. Morose   b. Depreciation   c. Blithe   d. Augur

__C__ 14. Ghost
   a. Ignominiously   b. Alienate   c. Apparition   d. Blithe

__C__ 15. Gloomily
   a. Fain   b. Consigned   c. Disconsolately   d. Obsequious

__D__ 16. Lacking reverence, respect or dutifulness
   a. Ague   b. Incongruity   c. Execrating   d. Impiously

__B__ 17. Domineeringly; overbearingly
   a. Felicitous   b. Imperiously   c. Epistle   d. Intricacies

__D__ 18. By accident or chance
   a. Approbation   b. Presentiment   c. Connubial   d. Fortuitously

__D__ 19. Make a statement of facts
   a. Futile   b. Truculent   c. Felicitous   d. Depose

__D__ 20. Denounced
   a. Detrimental   b. Asunder   c. Felicitous   d. Execrated

VOCABULARY WORKSHEET 2 - *Great Expectations*

___ 1. LATENT   A. Lucky

___ 2. FIDELITY   B. Forcefully; passionately

___ 3. PERVADE   C. Bringing out; drawing forth

___ 4. PERNICIOUS   D. Rooms where meals are served

___ 5. PERUSED   E. Tendencies

___ 6. OBSTINATELY   F. Supported by other evidence

___ 7. FELICITOUS   G. Summary

___ 8. EPISTLE   H. Faithfulness; loyalty

___ 9. CORROBORATED   I. Be present throughout

___ 10. REFECTORIES   J. Make a preliminary investigation

___ 11. IMPETUOSITY   K. At odds; not matching

___ 12. SYNOPSIS   L. Present but not active; hidden

___ 13. INCONGRUITY   M. Entrusted; gave over to the care of another

___ 14. ELICITING   N. Full of or showing servile compliance

___ 15. PROPENSITIES   O. Hint

___ 16. RECONNOITRE   P. Destructive; deadly

___ 17. INDELIBLE   Q. Stubbornly

___ 18. INTIMATION   R. Letter

___ 19. OBSEQUIOUS   S. Permanent

___ 20. CONSIGNED   T. Looked over with care

KEY: VOCABULARY WORKSHEET 2 - *Great Expectations*

L	1. LATENT	A. Lucky
H	2. FIDELITY	B. Forcefully; passionately
I	3. PERVADE	C. Bringing out; drawing forth
P	4. PERNICIOUS	D. Rooms where meals are served
T	5. PERUSED	E. Tendencies
Q	6. OBSTINATELY	F. Supported by other evidence
A	7. FELICITOUS	G. Summary
R	8. EPISTLE	H. Faithfulness; loyalty
F	9. CORROBORATED	I. Be present throughout
D	10. REFECTORIES	J. Make a preliminary investigation
B	11. IMPETUOSITY	K. At odds; not matching
G	12. SYNOPSIS	L. Present but not active; hidden
K	13. INCONGRUITY	M. Entrusted; gave over to the care of another
C	14. ELICITING	N. Full of or showing servile compliance
E	15. PROPENSITIES	O. Hint
J	16. RECONNOITRE	P. Destructive; deadly
S	17. INDELIBLE	Q. Stubbornly
O	18. INTIMATION	R. Letter
N	19. OBSEQUIOUS	S. Permanent
M	20. CONSIGNED	T. Looked over with care

VOCABULARY REVIEW GAME CLUES - *Great Expectations*

SCRAMBLED	WORD	CLUE
USUPUCOLRNSU	UNSCRUPULOUS	Without a conscience or a moral code
GAURU	AUGUR	Predict
AENCYEAB	ABEYANCE	Condition of being temporarily set aside
DSIGNECNO	CONSIGNED	Entrusted; gave over to the care of another
NMEUATDEG	AUGMENTED	Added to
HETIT	TITHE	One tenth
IATECTONNNOSR	CONSTERNATION	State of paralyzing dismay
SIOUOD	ODIOUS	Arousing strong dislike
DYUASSTII	ASSIDUITY	Constant personal attention
UROATEBD	OBDURATE	Hard-hearted; not giving into persuasion
OIUIETFLSC	FELICITOUS	Lucky
ANCENTNECSOU	COUNTENANCES	Faces
NEXDEARETO	EXONERATED	Freed from blame
NSNMGIOUMAA	MAGNANIMOUS	Generous in forgiving; noble
OIUCPYLESRSLUI	SUPERCILIOUSLY	Showing haughty disdain
PTSILEE	EPISTLE	Letter
YLSUOINIMIGNO	IGNOMINIOUSLY	Shamefully; humiliatingly
NEELTDRTMIA	DETRIMENTAL	Damaging
LATEIENA	ALIENATE	Turn away; push away
LSYOUGCAIAS	SAGACIOUSLY	Intelligently; wisely
YFIITELD	FIDELITY	Faithfulness; loyalty
CEDEATEXR	EXECRATED	Denounced
UTSYOFLRIUTO	FORTUITOUSLY	By accident or chance
OIRACUPCSI	CAPRICIOUS	Whimsical
TFEUIL	FUTILE	Having no useful result
YUITEOIMPTS	IMPETUOSITY	Forcefully; passionately
AITTAXEDEPR	EXPATRIATED	Removed from residence in one's native land
IDPTALE	PLAITED	Braided
OUUSAIPCSI	AUSPICIOUS	Marked by success; grand
SNOOCTRDE	CONSORTED	Associated
RNSUADE	ASUNDER	Apart from each other
NTLGIIEIC	ELICITING	Bringing out; drawing forth
RIAEODNEIPCT	DEPRECIATION	Belittling
RCNIOUTYNIG	INCONGRUITY	At odds; not matching

TNMLNAAGI	MALIGNANT	Disposed towards evil
AUOBNLCNI	CONNUBIAL	Relating to marriage
AMINTTOINI	INTIMATION	Hint
NTPOTNOIEM	OMNIPOTENT	All-powerful
OOTEACRRDBOR	CORROBORATED	Supported by other evidence
DCILU	LUCID	Easily understood
UPDREES	PERUSED	Looked over with care
NRIPTAOAOBP	APPROBATION	Approval
GARIVNELIP	PREVAILING	Most common